HEY WHITE MAN, HOW MUCH LONGER?

Overturning White Supremacy
and Asserting Racial Equality

Dr. Francis Hinga Lahai

HEY WHITE MAN, HOW MUCH LONGER?
OVERTURNING WHITE SUPREMACY AND
ASSERTING RACIAL EQUALITY

iUniverse books may be ordered through booksellers or by contacting:

iUniverse
1663 Liberty Drive
Bloomington, IN 47403
www.iuniverse.com
844-349-9409

ISBN: 978-1-6632-3698-2 (sc)
ISBN: 978-1-6632-3699-9 (e)

Library of Congress Control Number: 2022904898

Print information available on the last page.

iUniverse rev. date: 03/18/2022

To my wife, Ashmiru Jeneba Lahai, who has always reminded me that I am the son of the Most High God, the God who made all men equal.

To my daughter, Christiana, and my sons, Emmanuel and Jeffrey, you have encouraged me all the way—and your encouragement has made sure I give it all it takes to finish what I have started.

CONTENTS

PREFACE

THIS BOOK IS WRITTEN TO CONTRIBUTE TO THE EXISTING discussions about race, racism, discrimination, and racial inequality—discussions that have polarized many societies and even led to wars. It debunks some arguments in *Why Nations Fail* and explains the causes of African poverty and the future demise of White supremacy from an African perspective.

Many people have presented arguments that race-based prejudiced persons often use skin color as a signifier of identity and superiority of race. This illusion has become so deeply entrenched that races, including the Caucasian race or the "White man" have demonized the dark skin to the extent that they feel there will never be a match between the varying skin hues. No matter how poor a light-skinned person is or how inefficient they are, the light-skinned person is still treated better by his race kin than a successful dark-skinned person or boss. Added to that, skin color has become a significant trait in the Western world to determine who gets employed, who gets convicted, and who gets elected (*New York Times*, 2010).

In this book, the words White man, Caucasian, Whites, Black man, Blacks, Negro, Africans, Indo-Chinese, Yellow man, and

Asians are all used interchangeably but not to degrade any race. This is done with the anticipation that these terminologies will cease to serve as criteria for evaluation and judgment in the near future and to also have various readers identify with the content more easily.

The book goes through what I faced growing up in the southern towns of Moyamba and Bo, in Sierra Leone, West Africa in the 1960s, when the British Empire was slowly lowering the Union Jack in most of its colonial capital cities in the world, and the British influence was waning.

The centuries-old experience in the continents of Africa and Asia had already left a negative legacy that continues to have an impact on the social and economic position of Blacks in the world. The British and the Spanish, for example, succeeded in creating an elitist society for Europeans and a poor and slavish one for Blacks and Indo-Chinese.

In 1961, after a prolonged battle with the colonial administration for independence, Sierra Leone was granted freedom/independence, and the colony took over the administration. They collected taxes and accepted the responsibility of self-rule. The British Empire granted independence to its colonies and replaced it with indirect rule. The masters at the very top positions, like governors and district commissioners, governed using locals who had been trained as clerks and head teachers in schools at the lower cadres of administration. In French countries, on the other hand, a system of *assimilation* was introduced in which all were said to be *equal*, and Blacks and Whites could intermingle.

⊗ My Initial Experiences with Racism

My father, Samuel Saidu Lahai was a middle-class forestry officer, and he was among the few educated people who worked closely with the administration. We lived in a government clerks' quarters that was meant for junior and senior staff. The colonial schools had very strict White inspectors of schools, and the locals never wanted to fall short in their administrative duties for fear of being sacked. That administration encouraged dissent that prevented the locals from uniting in opposition. By so doing, the White colonial master established multiple points of contact for information and support. There were basically three groups: the first group consisted of the good-performing Blacks who were chosen to lead based on their success in education, the rich Blacks who had established farms and businesses, and the locals who had no choice but to cooperate with the White masters—no matter what. The second group acted as middlemen for the colonial masters, and as such, their children were given better education because they were open to scholarship opportunities to study overseas. The third group were just ordinary citizens.

For the colonial master, outsmarting the Blacks and becoming victorious and superior at the end was the ultimate goal. This included various tactics like repression, unfair access to information, unequal wages, and conditions of service and elimination of perceived natural Black leaders. As such, policy objectives were to be met at all costs, and there was hardly any place for failure. Therefore, performance targets were set, roles were defined, appraisals were done, and the results were used as necessary. This divisive approach thrived and was used all over the world. Blacks and the Indo-Chinese often blackmailed each other for such favors. All the kings and queens of Europe wanted was relative peace in the colonies and royalties paid to the king's or queen's court. Once these conditions were met, the king or queen allowed the governors to have their field day.

My father was among the last generation of elites who worked directly with the colonial masters before Sierra Leone gained her independence in 1961. Other prominent elites of the time included the likes of Dr. Sir Milton Margai, Albert Margai, Siaka Stevens, Dr. Sorie Fornah, to name but a few.

After working for the White colonialists for about a century, this bunch of civil servants came to realize that the colonialists were men just like them, and they dropped their inferiority complex, thinking that if the Whites could rule the colony relying on them, they could probably do better in the same positions the White colonialists had occupied for decades. These men thought they better understood their people and their culture to handle their matters well. With that in mind, they sought independence.

Other West African and Asian countries did the same, and the Blacks and the Indo-Chinese sought the right to rule their countries. The color of the skin did not matter because these countries needed more than just race relations, particularly when the British had used their youngest and middle-aged to run the affairs of the colonies, leaving out the most experienced and skilled people in Europe. It turned out that these young British governors were no match for the seasoned African leaders and paramount chiefs.

As custodians of the lore of the land, the paramount chiefs were members of the African royal families, chosen from a rigorous competition between ruling houses within the chiefdom. As a result, the paramount chiefs had the clout to mobilize their people and get positive results. My father was one of such elites. He married the daughter of a paramount chief and was confident that things would change one fine day. With that hope, he put us through the best schools and always reminded us about that. Today, I see that education is the key that unlocks doors to very high places—no matter how low you come from.

I attended a Roman Catholic primary school, headed by a White man, Father Patrick Moore. Father Moore was of the Jesuit Order and was in charge of the Saint Francis Primary School in Bo. He showed great interest in me due to excellent class results and good behavior, and he appointed me as an altar boy at age eight. All the altar boys cleaned the church on Saturdays and prepared to serve on the altar on Sundays. It was an enviable position, reserved for only the most well-behaved and most disciplined schoolboys.

At that tender age, I saw the organizational skills of the White man. Though these were missionaries, they had similar traits to the colonial masters, having had similar upbringing and training. The missionaries were disciplined, but the colonial masters protected and considered them counterparts who used religion, evangelism, education, and health systems to subjugate the locals.

Our foods, climate, and the freedom to intermingle made Sierra Leone an appealing place. At the time, there was no perceived racial inequality, and there was mutual respect. The reverend fathers worked on saving the souls of the locals, and they reciprocated by sending regular gifts and offerings and inviting them to visit their homes as part of their missionary work. Discrimination and racism developed over time as one race began to feel and exercise dominance. Over time, this became entrenched, which led to a cultural rift.

In 1971, I passed the Selective Entrance Examinations and proceeded to Christ the King College, another Catholic school in Bo, to continue my secondary education. The reverend fathers were in charge of the school. Strict discipline was enforced, timeliness and order were imposed, and the teaching materials were of the highest grade. These were the hallmarks of quality education.

Whenever there was competition between the secondary schools in Bo City, the "college boys," as we were referred to, would be asked to behave themselves and respect the authority of whoever was arbitrating. That made us accept any results—good or bad. It sent the message around the country that CKC was a good school, and it attracted the best brains and the sons of the country's elites.

The school attracted a class of international teachers from India, the UK, and the United States. I began to see a correlation between peace, diligence, and development. CKC was doing better academically than its rival schools—the Bo School, Ahmadiyya Secondary School, and United Christian Council (UCC) School—because of its strict discipline. We felt and looked different. We developed the cockiness characterized by the elitist group of schools, in line with the likes of the Grammar School, Annie Walsh, and the Prince of Wales Schools in the capital city, Freetown.

By the 1980s, things started to change as the reverend fathers became more entrenched. As the character of the Whites in relation to their perceived superiority evolved, events at the schools changed too. They deviated from their mandate of inculcating religious and moral standards of racial equality in their pupils. They were bold enough to insult locals and become involved in activities that were incompatible with their status. Their respect for the local people waned, and some had to be sent back to Ireland and Italy.

Upon completion of my secondary education, I spent a year teaching, and I eventually got a scholarship to study in the People's Republic of China. Two of us were selected from an intense competition of more than two hundred students. Arriving in China, we took ten months to learn the Mandarin Chinese language. China has sixty-six ethnic groups, but the Han—who speak the commonly known Mandarin—are the largest. Their language is now the lingua franca of the People's Republic of China. This was enforced by Mao Zedong, the first chairman of the Communist Party, as a way of unifying the country.

Putonghua ("common language" in Chinese) is easier to write than its complicated Cantonese equivalent. We did our best, and within ten months, we were ready to enter university to do engineering. I impressed my friends and family by being so quick to learn how to speak and write the language. However, we were not admitted into the same class as the Americans and Europeans. Classification was by cultural and socioeconomic backgrounds. They also paid higher tuition fees and had different kinds of teachers.

By the tenth month, the Africans were speaking better Chinese and writing better Chinese. We were then accorded the same opportunity, and that amazed me. For the first time, I had the chance to sit under similar examination conditions as the White man—the race that my father was so terrified of—and I was doing better than they were doing.

In June 1983, I got my diploma in Chinese language, and I was accepted into the Nanjing Southeast University (then Nanjing Institute of Technology) to study civil engineering. At the Beijing

Language Institute (now Beijing Languages University), I developed confidence in myself and was not deterred by color. If I did better than the White students, I was convinced the same should happen for the Chinese.

We thought we would be treated with some compassion in class with the Chinese because of having only one year of the language, and we thought the lecturers would understand that we were not born Chinese. They never did, and I became worried. I could never understand why there was so much pressure.

I was so afraid of sitting in class with the Chinese students, and at some point, I developed a fever. I was used to being in the top five of my class, and I did not know how I could handle a lesser position. Since childhood, my father had made me appreciate each "excellent" result I came home with. I had a phobia of being at the bottom.

Some of my senior foreign students from Yemen, Palestine, and Sri Lanka told me not to panic. "Just study hard—and whatever you get in the examinations is fine," they said.

I heeded their advice, and I soon started getting better results—better than even the Chinese students in class. One of the lecturers, a female and staunch nationalist, got upset and could not hide her emotions. She told the Chinese students in class that they had to be ashamed of themselves for having an African student beat them in class. "You needed to work harder and make our country proud," she shouted.

The lecturer did not know that I had been among the best back home and had gotten my scholarship through a highly competitive process. She didn't know that I had been fondly called "Chike Obi the Young Mathematician," "Maada," and "the wise old man." Some even called me "Doctor Dynamite," exploding everywhere and bringing about positive change. I was their own Einstein. We had other academic giants and brains in Sierra Leone too.

I still laugh at the Chinese lecturer's ranting, and at the time, with my fading inferiority complex, I still wondered how a dark-skinned man could beat the light-skinned man in examinations. In

Nanjing, at the age of nineteen, I had confirmed for myself that it was very possible for a Black man to excel in examinations—even more than the White man and the Indo-Chinese combined. It was the first proof, to me, that skin color does not matter when it comes to intellectual prowess. Later, I found out that the same idea was being established in Europe and the Americas.

So, what was it that made the White man feel they were more superior? It was a question that I initially found difficult to answer, but my experience at the university provided me with some answers. I came to realize that it was an illusion that was developed over time by one group of humanity. I came to realize that it was not a collective race of people who were more superior than the other races; it was a few individuals, mostly from one race, who feel and act superior to other few individuals in another race. If the aggregate figures are higher on one side, the claim becomes seemingly legitimate.

The related question is whether America's industrial might would be complete without Indo-Chinese and African American input. A superficial answer to this is no. It's like saying that Nigeria would not need Caucasian migrant workers to fuel its labor force. Or are all the inventions from the space agency, NASA, the result of only the Caucasians? Do the battle victories of General Colin Powell—with other Caucasian Whites—make the Black race superior? Was it not the United States, as a nation, that achieved overall superiority? Such are the questions that keep pricking my mind. Logically, these would have required straight yes-or-no answers, but rationally, they would not, and this makes race or color, as a signifier, untenable—at least not for the White man.

In the chapters that follow, we will debunk the ideology of White supremacy under equal conditions of existence. We will show that the integrated nature of the world economy cannot allow for a single race to claim superiority over other races any longer. This also will prove the assertion that all men were created equal, and it is the efforts of an individual and the environment they find themselves in that make the difference. This status quo is just temporary, and where the factors that elevated one to a more superior rank are not properly managed and one loses control, this status will change. Britain and France lost their global hegemony to the United States and Russia at some point. The kingdoms of Cush, Ashanti, and Zimbabwe all lost their supremacy at some point. I then asked, "Hey, White man, what makes you think you will stay superior forever? How much longer?"

PART ONE

My world in Which Africa Is about Left Out—and the Whites Are Falling

CHAPTER ONE

The Origins of Man

O F THE EARTH'S DISCOVERIES, MAN IS THE MOST INTELLIGENT. Not even the greatest inventions in science compare to man's fearful make.

Historically, human beings have lived on planet Earth long enough to be able to adequately pass judgment about its make and nature. Yet, assumptions about the Earth and its peoples by many scholars remain a vexing issue to many other scholars. Two dominating theories relate directly to the topic of the discussion, which have made the best attempts at explaining the complexity of the Earth. One relates to the lack of data or historical artefacts that can adequately support the claims by some scholars regarding the Earth, given the span of time covered by these theories. Another claim is that the clay remains or the bones of ancient men did not survive.

This section presents some key examples of these opinions and theories, including ideas about race relations on Earth.

⊗ Religious Creationary Origins of Man

There are many religions in the world, each having an account of how humans came to planet Earth and how the relationship with other species is supposed to be. A majority of men and women belong to five major religions, including the nonbelievers: Buddhism (7.2 percent), Christianity (32.5 percent), Hinduism (13.8 percent), indigenous religions (11.8 percent), Islam (22.5 percent), Judaism (0.2 percent), and nonreligious people/atheists/agnostics (11.8 percent). The Figure 1 below shows the distribution of these major religions around the world. While Christianity continues to remained the dominant religion of the world in 2010, Islam is growing fast and gaining influence in the Middle East and Africa.

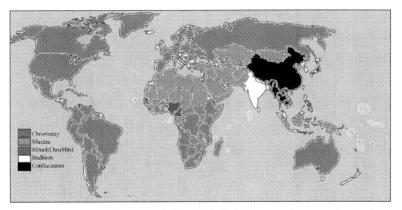

Figure 1: Distribution of the World's Religions (Source: Author)

Of the five major religions, three are monotheistic, believing in one God who created the Earth. These are Judaism, Christianity, and Islam. The others, such as Buddhism and Hinduism, are polytheistic, believing that several gods are responsible for varied aspects of human life.

The Bible and Quran claim the world was created by God Almighty and that He (God) first created man. Though these books do not explicitly give a date for the creation of the world, it can be inferred from the Bible, in the era of the tower of Babel and Egyptian predynastic era (6000 BCE) to modern day (AD 2000) that humankind has inhabited the Earth for only close to eight thousand years, beginning with the accounts of the prophet Moses in the book of Genesis to the present day. This makes it different from the evolutionary theory in which the Earth is millions of years old and humans are said to be hundreds of thousands of years old with the discovery of the fossil of Lucy, the oldest human ancestor.

Specifically, Genesis 1:26 states that God created man, called Adam, and from Adam's ribs, He created a supportive second being, the woman, whom He called Eve. Eve became the wife of Adam, the first man. In this account, there is neither a mention of the color of the man's skin nor that of the woman. However, the Bible makes it clear that man started to exist the day he was made in a garden, called Eden. In the Edenic garden, man and woman disobeyed their Maker. They disobeyed God's laws, and they were banished from the garden where they initially knew no shame, had no pride, and lived by what God instructed.

Adam and Eve had two children, Cain and Abel, after they repented. Cain was a farmer who killed his animal-rearing brother, Abel, because he was jealous. It was not because of the skin color of his brother. It was because God accepted the offering of Abel and rejected his. There was no mention made or suggested of the difference in skin color as the reason for the jealousy. It was about character and understanding what God required at the time. Details of this sordid story can be read from the Bible in Genesis 4.

From that point on, Cain started a nomadic life. Adam and Eve had other children who had their own children, and they contributed to populate the ancient world. These children, grandchildren, and great-grandchildren all came from the same parents. They were brothers and sisters or otherwise related. They saw each other as one family and coinhabited the available lands. Nothing about superiority relating to skin color—or differences as a result of that— was mentioned.

As time went on, some members of the family began to migrate in search of more space and greener pastures. They moved away from the Garden of Eden and went to distant lands where they further multiplied. Today, we have a world with a population of about seven billion people of four or five predominant races.

⊗ Where Exactly Is the Garden of Eden Located?

Historical and archaeological records have proposed that the garden of Eden was located between Iraq and Jordan. The fact that the Bible account says that "The Lord placed a flaming sword at the gate" means the biblical God never wanted anyone to discover the exact location of the garden. Worse still, the worldwide flood talked about in the Bible—occurring several hundred years later in the regions mentioned here—helps obliterate all traces of the exact location of the garden.

From a biblical perspective, humans came from Jordan, Iraq, or Africa. Why is Africa mentioned? The oldest human bones ever discovered were discovered in Africa. *Homo sapiens* and Lucy, discovered in Africa, could not have migrated from distant lands to Africa. The rest of humankind, therefore, are descendants of the oldest humans, Africans or Arabs.

The issue of superiority did not arise then, and the White man should not pride themselves on always being superior to the Black man. In an African context, the okra tree cannot be greater than the master (the person who planted it). Except in acquiring wealth and materials, can we say that the White man is more skilled than the Black man? That does not, by any means, make him superior. We will come back to this subject of superiority later in the book.

⊗ Evolutionary Origins of Man

In the early 1800s, Jean Baptiste Lamarck was the first person to write about the evolution theory of life. Aristotle and others had slowly deviated from the theology that life originates from God and proposed a more secular theory that species evolve over time—in a sense that apes were the advanced evolutionary form of sea creatures that migrated to land.

In 1827, Ernst Haeckel (1744–1829) published *On the Evolution of life*. He illustrated a "tree of life" where man was at the pinnacle, starting from little creatures as the abiogenesis (one-celled living creature) to small creatures as amoeba that slowly evolved over time into crawling creatures. The evolutionary circle kept spinning until we had four-legged animals, and then we had creatures like gorillas, chimpanzees, and baboons that stood on two legs and two forelimbs. At the final evolutionary stage, modern man was formed. Modern man had the quality of being intelligent, fast to move, and had shorter arms than his predecessor. However, no conclusive, evidence-based explanation is available to provide the reason why evolution stopped with man or why this evolutionary process is not happening any longer in any part of the world. Why were huge mammals like elephants not evolving but only developed from birth in a complete shape?

In 1858, Charles Darwin, a British biologist, published *On the Evolution of Species*. He described how natural selection in evolution makes provision for species that have evolved from the same base cells to be different from their kin by the next evolutionary stage. Trees, plants, animals, and humans could be different in form and shape after evolution to have different types of bananas, different types of fishes, and different races, for example. In the same way, races of people must have evolved from a single cell that divided into different colors with similar forms: two legs, two eyes, one nose, yet having the same red blood cells. If this is something to go by, then we can safely say that while Darwin was actually copying ideas from the *creationist theory*, his natural selection ideas showed that White, Black, and Indo-Chinese people evolved from the same amoebic cell. Except for the fundamental dysfunctions in cell reproduction over time, this opinion can be held as being true. However, this is not observed to be the same for billions of people in the world today. Internal body organs from the other races with matching blood samples have been used all over the world, yielding good results. This means that one race can safely use any organ from any other race.

Darwin's theory does not propose that there are superior races, but it says there are differences in genetic makeups that evolve over time, which have made certain species more resilient to their natural environments. This gave birth to the popular theory of *survival of the fittest*. This explains why some people survive in malaria-prone areas and why others survive in cold climates. Some are fitter in tropical environment, and others are fitter in temperate climates or the tundra. What in the end clearly juts out is that species from the same environments respond in the same or similar way to stimulus, and if these races were interchanged, over time, the new arrivals would adjust to their new environment. No particular area of the world was made for particular races. Africans have survived for centuries in Northern America, and Whites have survived in Africa. This partly proves the equality of the makeup of the races.

Here again, the question about superiority does not arise.

Reflections

The wild beasts will honour me, the jackals and the ostriches, for I give water in the wilderness and rivers in the desert, to give drink to my chosen people, the people whom I formed for myself that they might declare my praise.
—Isaiah 43:20

The strength of the crocodile is in the water—meaning people can be very strong in their right environments.
—African proverb

Overcoming poverty is not a task of charity, it is an act of justice. Like slavery and apartheid, poverty is not natural. It is man-made and it can be overcome and eradicated by the actions of human beings. Sometimes it falls on a generation to be great. You can be that great generation. Let your greatness blossom.
—Nelson Mandela

CHAPTER TWO

The Concept of the Supremacy of the Races

RACISM PREACHES THAT PEOPLE OF ONE COLOR OF SKIN ARE better than others of different colors and that those with White skin are the most superior. The definition of "White" actually varies from country to country, and the impression of racism is felt more in countries where a majority of one skin-colored people are living together. This heterogeneity is the case in South Africa, the United States of America, Brazil, Myanmar, India, and a few more.

From the experience of the author, it is observed that there is usually less racism in homogeneous-skinned developing countries than in homogenous-skinned developed countries. In developing countries, there is a tendency to admire lighter-skinned persons rather than looking at them as superior. The same applies in developed societies where, to a certain level, there is admiration for light skin. In Asian countries, the history and religion long preached—even before the advent of the Black man—that black was bad luck or not desirable and white was good. In this, women are more inclined to love light skin than men who generally are dark-skinned due to their love for exterior work and the exposure to longer periods of sunlight.

Merriam Webster defines supremacy as "the quality or state of having more power, authority, or status than anyone else." In the limited opinion of some White folks, they see themselves as being better placed in society than their African or Asian hominoids. These stereotyping of self is closely related to social construction of the mentality of these groups of people. This was reinforced after travels to faraway lands just after the industrial revolution when traveling was facilitated by faster engines.

In South Africa, the classification of race is simply in three categories: Black, White, and Colored (mixed or Asian descent). The Brazilian definition goes further and creates five races. The races in Brazil are a mix of skin color and social status. They include *Indigenes* otherwise known as Amerindians, *Pretos* (Black), *Brancos* (White), *Pardos* (multiracial), *Caboclos,* and *Mamelucos* and *Amerelos* (Asians). While the Caboclos and Mamelucos are mixed Amerindian and White, the Black and White mixture is called *Mulatto.*

The term *mulatto* developed in the 1870 census in the United States as more farm owners saw no boundary between Black and White and started wooing their slave women and vice versa. The young White women loved the passionate way the Black men dealt with them and often conceived mulattoes to the chagrin of the White parents. Some babies were murdered or left abandoned so that the stigma of Black association was lost. Other Whites abandoned their White lineage to raise the poor baby mulattoes, and in so doing, the population of mulattoes grew to their present levels in the United States, South America, Europe, and South Africa.

White supremacy or White supremacism is the belief that White people are superior to people of other races and therefore should be dominant over them. This has led to several definitions of the White man. However, prior to the 1700s when the concept started gaining ground, several civilizations had in one way or another developed racial segregations and displayed superiority.

Throughout history, certain groups of people have claimed superiority over small groups and clans until the White race grew into a worldwide movement of like-skinned people claiming superiority. These included the following groups of Whites, Blacks and Asian peoples: the Israelites, the Romans, the British, the Nazis of Adolf Hitler and the Aryans, the Boers in apartheid, the Ku Klux Klan, and the Shona in Shaka Zulu's homeland. On the other side of the spectrum, the Blacks also had superior cultures like in Timbuktu, Zimbabwe, and Ashanti.

In this scenario where skin color was not the only determinant of race, successful Blacks and Amerindian chiefs and people of class in the other races were respected and given higher social status, being treated differently from those of lower social class. All they did was change the perspective society had of them through their achievements, and they moved up the social or economic ladder.

South Africans Leonard Thompson and Martin Legassick wrote *Foreign Investment and the Reproduction of Racial Capitalism in South Africa*. They believed the idea of White supremacy began from mythology and from the economic performance of Whites more than from ethnic divisions. In the early stages, several reasons for segregation were proposed, and then the full-blown concept of apartheid and race distinction eventually settled in and became institutionalized.

Racial segregation in South Africa started as a way of maintaining social order and control over Blacks. The classification of society ensured cheaper labor was available through lower wages and fewer perks. Over time, the institutions of segregation became a social construction with the ultimate effect of creating resentment among the disadvantaged for the benefit of the "Whites."

In 2000, the United States Census Bureau made it clear that the classification of peoples within the country was not based on scientific or anthropological backgrounds but on "social and cultural characteristics as well as ancestral background." This is where the law seems to condone the socially constructed norm and makes racism and segregation legal. However, the same law that allows citizens to declare which race they more closely relate to would not allow a Black mulatto to declare themselves White. This would be hysterical. The appearance of Black parentage in the bloodstream invalidates all rights to Whiteness. Whiteness has now been described as for persons of European, Middle Eastern, and North African origin and includes Syrians, Lebanese, and Russians as long as they can pretend to understand and live the White American lifestyle.

A closer study of the race definitions in the United States shows that the definition of Whiteness has been fluid and best reflects the tolerance that the first White settlers had for other citizens. While the Mexicans are neighbors to the Americans and are sometimes classed as White, the others from South America are Hispanics. They are considered a mix of Spanish, Portuguese, African, and Amerindian. There could be White or Black Hispanics and with that comes perceived differences in how they are received and treated in various forums by the White and Blacks.

Johann Friedrich Blumenbach (1752–1840) devised another classification of races and focused on regional spread of the majority of persons of similar physical traits. His was based on the cranial formation and other characteristics like hair, eye color, and skin color. In 1779, he proposed five races:

- the Caucasian race (Europe, the Caucasus, Asia Minor, North Africa, and West Asia)
- the Mongolian race (East Asia, Central Asia, and South Asia)
- the Aethiopian race (West Africa, Central Africa, South Africa, East Africa, including the Horn of Africa, and Australia)
- the American race (North America and South America)
- the Malayan race (Southeast Asia)

The Caucasian race is now widely referred to as the White race, whereas the Mongolian race is the Asian race or Upper Indo-Chinese race. The Aethiopian race is referred to as the Negro or African race, and the American race is the Amerindian race. The Malayan race is the Lower Indo-Chinese race. These classifications are the most widely accepted around the world. As the human race has developed over the ages, there has been a move from clans to urban societies.

In the clan system, people of similar backgrounds—such as skin color, culture, and language—would be linked together and bonded for decades and sometimes centuries. There is a feeling today that the White supremacists may have developed their ideologies from clanship. The need for self-assurance and comfort among members of a clan has led to a prolonged period of coexistence and eventually a new defined culture of Whiteness.

In some regions, the indigenous peoples created monumental architecture, large-scale organized cities, city-states, chiefdoms, states, kingdoms, and empires. Among these are the Aztec, Inca, and Maya states that until the sixteenth century were among the most politically and socially advanced nations in the world. They had a vast knowledge of engineering, architecture, mathematics, astronomy, writing, physics, medicine, planting and irrigation, geology, mining, sculpture, and goldsmithing.

According to other sociologists, a human can be classified based on combinations of appearance, such as skin color and shade, stature, facial features, hair color and texture, head form, nose shape, eye color and shape, height, and blood or gene type. People associate with others of similar features. However, attempts have been made by scientists to racially classify people and prevent intermarriages in other cases.

In South Africa, the United States, Germany, Brazil and the UK, three reasons for classification were developed. Firstly, mixing of the races in intermarriages caused weaker new races. "Mulattoes" were especially victims of this classification. Further marriages of mulattoes could lead to even weaker species.

Another possibility raised by Charles Benedict Davenport, Gregor Mendel, Glayde Whitney, and others were that the offspring could partly develop the genes of one race and partly the other genes of the other race and so have a genetic mismatch or genetic disharmony. In such a case, if a tall parent from North Europe married to a shorter southern European, there would be mismatch of physical organs. However, over a century of these intermarriages or concubines, offspring have proven all these theories wrong. The body perfectly adjusts to the new offspring and ensures a healthy body if the ideal nutrients are provided from birth. Personalities of mixed races, like Colin Powell, Reverend Jesse Jackson, and others, have lived beyond seventy years of age and are examples that these assertions are not true. Even today, there are attempts to discourage racial intermarriages on political grounds.

Secondly, the process of evolution could be compromised if racial groups were allowed to intermingle. In this case, it would be ideal to keep the races apart as groupings of people. Some anthropologists even believe that this group separation was a natural tendency of human personalities and maintaining gene pools as one of the basic pillars of modern civilization.

Thirdly, the widespread belief propagated is that the races are genetically so different that some are endowed with superior qualities and personalities than others. As such the well-endowed groups with superior cognitive and behavioral traits should not intermingle but be treated as superior to the others and so be separated.

These unsubstantiated scientific results have been used against Blacks, the Indo-Chinese, some Europeans, and Jews throughout history with brute force. Science has been a quiet accomplice in the perpetration of these ills.

United States Navy Admiral William McRaven, in his famous "If You Want to Change the World, Start Off by Making Your Bed" speech, noted that nothing matters in life but the will to succeed—not the color of your skin, your ethnic background, your education, or your social status. He went on to say that if you want to change the world, do not judge a person by the color of their skin, their ethnic background, or their social status. He admonished the new recruits to measure people by the size of their hearts and not by the size of their flippers. Everyone can succeed in life if there is a strong will and support. He finally admonished that if they want to change the world, they should lift up the fallen.

This brilliant speech by an American passed through one ear of the graduates and came out the other because those same young recruits became the leaders of the United States—and they do not seem to remember his speech. The world would have been a better place if generations continued to remember Admiral McRaven and his likes. He may be racist, but he did not give that impression in his speech.

CHAPTER THREE

Racism among the Nations

I GREW UP IN SIERRA LEONE, ONE OF THE SMALLEST COUNTRIES IN the world and a very homogeneous race country, not knowing what racism was. My first experience with racism was with the Soweto Riots of 1971. In secondary school, we thought all countries in Africa had only Black people, and all non-Black people living in Sierra Leone were from Europe, China, India, Syria, or Lebanon. The Europeans were either colonial masters or missionaries. They never came to Africa on small retail business then. To us, it seemed like the Indo-Chinese and Arabs had arrived on the shores of Africa because of wars in their native countries, and they were looking for opportunities and refuge in far-flung countries of Africa where there were no extremes of racial prejudice, and opportunities for survival existed for all.

Suddenly, South Africa was in the news as having battles

between Black people and White People. The Soweto Riots and the arrest and imprisonment of Nelson Mandela made me interested in the makeup of South Africa. I read *Mine Boy, Cry Freedom,* and *Things Fall Apart*—by African writers—and I began to get a feel of what the Blacks and Indians were going through at the hands of a minority of White people who had come to believe that they were better placed to lead at all times.

By the time I got to secondary school in 1974, I was adopted by an White Englishman by the name of Michael Downham. Mike was very helpful to young Sierra Leoneans, and he worked hard all the time. He first came into the country and settled in Mattru Jong in the south as a science and chemistry teacher in secondary schools. He built relationship with all and minded his own business. Though he lived a better life and had an expatriate salary, he never showed any signs of superiority over the other teachers. When it came to academics, he would show his superior knowledge by bringing up theories that the local teachers had not learned. These were the only times I noticed "Donny," as he was fondly called, show that he had better training. It was rumored that he had a son in the UK, but due to differences with his wife, he preferred to run away to remote Africa than face the reality of a married life. This was different for us in Africa. A man must be a man! No matter the odds. How can a man run from a woman who was his wife? Mike Downham did not care who he lived among. He knew these were people like him—humans in every sense.

In the Catholic schools, we had mixed-race teachers including Indian, English, Irish, Sierra Leonean, Nigerian, and Black Americans. The students were mixed also since these expatriates had their children attending school with us. In these classes, Sierra Leoneans came top, and the expatriate children did very well. We played football and volleyball together. It looked like we were all the same people. We had fun and laughed at common jokes.

However, in a match one afternoon, Val Boyer, a White American boy, ran so fast that he fell down and bruised himself badly. He was crying and blood was oozing out of his skin. We all shouted, "He has red blood." We had been used to walking, running, and laughing together, but to see Val crying and having the same color of blood inside was a shock. So, what made these White-skinned people any different? If they also had red blood and two noses and one mouth, two hands and two feet, then we must share a common heritage. We must be all hominoid. This question lingered in my mind for a long time. Later in Biology class we were to learn of pigments called Melanin in the Blacks which was less or lacking in light-skinned persons. So was it just melanin the cause of racism?

My research has come to tell me that race means different things to different people at different times in history and in different locations around the world. The idea of different races never really existed as a genetic classification until the 1700s. Prior to this, human perception of "the other" was controlled by religious thinking.

Christianity, Judaism, and Islam all preached equality of people. All men were created equal, in the image of a divine God, and no one was expected to look down on the others' ethnicity or class within particular geographic areas or continents. By the late 1700s, Europeans had invented the steam engine and could travel longer distances over land and sea and return to tell the stories. Marco Polo traveled to China and returned to Europe. David Livingstone traveled to East Africa and returned to tell of the diamonds and the source of the Nile. Others traveled to West Africa and discovered iron ore and diamonds. Christopher Columbus traveled to the Americas and met Indians. Sir Henry, the navigator, traveled to West Africa and other areas. These travels held the origins of modern slavery and racism.

According to the Harvard Institute for Economic Research on Ethnic Diversity, ethnicity and race are social constructs. This, in effect, means that the perceptions of people about a region vary depending on who they are dealing with. While the majority of African nations are very ethnically diverse, most of Europe and South America are perceived to not be very diverse except for the existence of multi-skin-colored peoples. The majority of people in these countries speak the same language, and foreigners who emigrate to these countries find its better to integrate, learn the language, and behave as the locals than to entirely maintain their native cultures if they are to better themselves. Still, racism and segregation are found in the midst of such culturally nondiverse communities. The United States has been classified as a middle level of diversity, and Canada is very diverse, but both are very pro-White in their thinking.

It was also observed that rich nations are highly homogeneous in race, culture, and thinking. In a situation of high economic benefits, immigrants have been known to change due to conflict and migration. Except for very resilient families, African Africans change to African Americans and Asians become Asian Americans. Demographic trends and other economic factors force White persons to become aligned with others of similar cultural backgrounds, and that is also the case for the Blacks. The question of Whiteness as a superior race is a mystery, and it is not as simple as a difference only in skin color.

The *Washington Post*'s Max Fisher published two maps from data gleaned from the World Values Survey (2019) and the Harvard Institute of Economic Research. The two maps show that most multiethnic countries are racially tolerant, and homogenous countries are less racially tolerant.

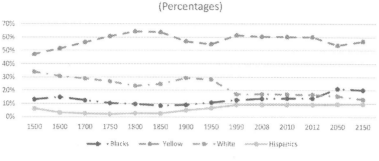

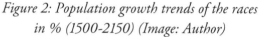

Figure 2: Population growth trends of the races
in % (1500-2150) (Image: Author)

⊗ **Mixing with Different Peoples**

The map below measures the scale to which residents of the country accept other ethnicities as their neighbors. It shows Canada is a very unique country with the highest diversity in the world but with also the most racially and culturally tolerant attitudes. Australia seems the direct opposite with a very homogenous culture that is also very racially tolerant. History, however, shows that the Whites of Australia have been very intolerant of the Aborigines, and only major legislation and large-scale migration of Asians has "forced" the Whites to become tolerant. It is almost as if the awareness is setting in that it is unfair that the indigenes met on their land can be losing all their rights while newer settlers are being allowed to enjoy the best of the land at the detriment of the aborigines. What could have sparked such sympathetic tendencies in the hearts of the other races toward the Blacks of Australia and New Zealand? Decades of campaigns from religious bodies and civil society seem to be paying off.

⊗ Racism in Communist China

Life in Communist China (between 1948 and 1990) is far different from the Two-Systems China (between 1990 and today). I will first look at some cases in Communist China and later in the chapter on superpower relations and racism in the Two-Systems China.

In 1983, I was fortunate to be among two Sierra Leoneans out of two hundred who vied for the scholarship to the People's Republic of China. While I was chosen for engineering studies, my countryman went for medicine. The Cold War between Western powers and China and the USSR was still ongoing. The system of one country with two-systems had just been launched in which socialism and capitalism could be allowed to work concurrently in China in a new open-door policy by Deng Xiao Ping ("Small Deng" as he was fondly called.

Deng Xiao Ping's and People's Republic of China's open-door policy catered to students from all over the world in various disciplines. It was meant to create opportunities to see China and be seen by the Chinese. As the leader after Mao Zedong, Deng realized that China could not completely eliminate capitalist practices and shut its doors to the world in its development without paying the price of inferior technologies and less market access. Market access included both developed and underdeveloped countries.

They went on to classify the world with Africa among the third world countries. They counted on them as "brothers and friends" in an effort to develop the Third World alliance and get international recognition as leader of a large group. There was no room for racism. It was a matter of survival, and the hard reality was that, properly developed, the relationship between Africa and China could change global economic dynamics. Africa was a source of raw materials, and China had middle-level industrialization. The products could be sold to the United States and Europe at cheaper prices, thereby beating Japan and the rest of Asia. So, the well-calculated scholarships were meant to start building a longer, stronger bridge between the Black continent and the Indo-Chinese subcontinent.

Unlike the UK's Commonwealth Scholarships or the American Fulbright Program, this new China approach was welcomed by developing countries since it applied to both undergraduate and postgraduate studies. See Figure 3.

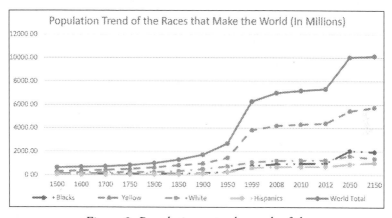

Figure 3: Population growth trends of the races in millions (Image: Author)

In September 1982, I traveled out of my country for the first time. My mother was devastated. I had been one of her favorite children. In a family of ten children, I was arguably the brightest. My elder brothers were doing well, and the family was well known in Bo City, but my results were different.

My mother wanted the development but not the separation. Who was going to be near her to help with the smaller kin? What lies overseas with the Whites? Will they take care of her beloved child? She wept so much that she never went to the airport to see me off as was the culture in those days.

When an elder brother, Moses, had left earlier for his PhD studies, she traveled from upcountry to Freetown and the airport. This was a four-day trip, leaving behind her business and the other smaller kin. For me, I assured her that I would be fine and would see her as soon as I completed my studies. Little did I realize that it would be twelve years before I would see her again.

While in Beijing Language Institute in 1982, I was fortunate to meet people of different races from all over the world. China was reopening to Western ideologies, and students came from Africa, Asia, Australia, Europe, the Middle East, the UK, and the United States, and we mingled with the local Chinese students. For the first time in my life, I was able to sit in class with so many diversely cultured students. We went to the same canteens, restaurants, nightclubs, and churches. It gave me the opportunity to measure levels of tolerance firsthand.

In the 1980s, every foreign student in China was being watched by unseen eyes for various reasons. For the Africans, it was mostly that they would not get mistreated at the hands of the Chinese locals. For the Europeans, there was more a fear of "spiritual pollution." Spiritual pollution was the idea that frequent direct contacts between Chinese and foreigners could lead them to lose their socialist ideologies and adopt Western ideologies of capitalism, free speech, free thinking, and sex equality.

My association with the Chinese students at the Beijing Languages Institute (Beijing Yuyan Xue Yuan) was more for academic pursuits so that I could learn the language faster and do well in my academics. It turned out that there were business opportunities also available that had not been exploited. Since the Chinese students and the population in general could not travel out of the country, they would not have access to better-quality clothes, shoes, and electronic gadgets. When one student visited my room, she noticed that I had the latest stereo double cassette player, just released by Sony and a video player. A television belonged to my roommate. She was amazed. She had been told, I later understood, that Africans had come to China because they could not help themselves and that the Chinese government was doing everything for them. This was not entirely true.

In the bilateral arrangements, the African students were offered tuition-free education and boarding by China—but required that their countries provide some support and their families do the rest. Once the Chinese students understood this, I noticed a marked change in perception of the Africans. Information and knowledge are power. No longer did they see the Africans as poor and beggarly; they were seen as intelligent, hardworking, and coming from respectable homes.

The other ideology propagated by college authorities was that we were sons and daughters of the cadre (*gan bu*) in our home countries and had privileged status to have gained the scholarships. This view of the Africans sometimes saved us from trouble. The locals saw us as diplomatic material and gave respect. In both situations, the common man looked at us with wary caution and as much as possible avoided any clashes.

I loved when we went shopping. In 1982, the People's Republic of China had introduced two currencies of the same value, but they were to be used at different locations. The *Wai Hui Bi* and the *Ren Min Bi*'s value were at par, but the *Wai Hui bi* was used in supermarkets and shops with foreign goods. In all local stores, you would use the local *Ren Min Bi*.

If a Chinese friend or classmate wanted foreign goods, they would talk to us. We would buy it for them and get reimbursed. Initially, this was difficult. There was fear of these exchanges being intercepted. However, sons and daughters of the *Gan Bu* were bolder. There was more intermingling and the fear or loathing of the Black man dissipated as they understood us better. With time, it partly confirmed the Chinese government's fear of spiritual pollution.

Most Africans either did not feel involved in spiritual pollution or the strategic implications of this ideology. To the African, this was unthinkable. We had been trained in a culture of freedom and enjoyment based on our means and in due consideration of the source of the pleasure. The Africans were not a priority target.

As more students were trained and more African diplomats came to China, living among the Chinese population, there was a better understanding of the relationships between Asian Chinese and

Africans and Europeans. Life became bearable without some of the luxuries of a free capitalist world. We understood Communism and Socialism better—but not enough to advocate for this system in our home countries. I think there was unanimous thinking by the Africans. Somehow, Tanzania experimented with socialism. As a support to the Tanzanian government, China built the Tanzania-Zambia railway (the Tazara), which is a lasting legacy of the start of their friendship.

At BLI, the Chinese students also came from different parts of China to learn foreign languages. Some had never met Blacks or Whites, and this was the arena for exchanges. As the ice broke between cultures in this cultural melting point, we were able to get firsthand insight into the thoughts about the races.

As we chatted one winter day, with sub-zero temperatures, I was cuddled up and looking at the leafless trees.

Suddenly, one of the Chinese girls sheepishly asked, "Hey, Francis, is it true that, in Africa, people live in trees?"

I was shocked for a moment, but I thought fast. I had been warned by other students that questions like these pop up every now and again among friends, but when it comes at you directly like this, there is always that surprise. My reply was already prepared. "Well, you know," I hesitated for a little while then continued, "the Chinese ambassador in our country actually lives in one of the biggest trees."

"No, but that's not possible," shot back my friend almost immediately.

"Why not? Well, if he cannot live in a tree, then no one lives in trees in Africa."

This made her go into a long and pensive silence. I realized they must have watched a movie of some pygmy families in the forests who would seek higher ground in rainy seasons and build houses in the trees. That laid that idea to rest in her mind. I am sure she shared this with many friends.

At the BLI, there were more than four thousand students. Two students were assigned per room. The institute was careful to combine students based on race: Africans to Africans, Asian to Asian, and so on. Occasionally, a European could be matched with a non-European White. Where there was a difference in religion, this soon posed a problem, and they would separate. Race relations was not just about skin color. They were also based on religion and economic integration.

Most of Africa was colonized by Europeans. The values and cultures of the Blacks and Whites have been shared in the south for more than five hundred years. Therefore, it was also noticed that Africans and Europeans got along well because of languages like English, French, Spanish and Portuguese. Within the first two years of my stay in China, I met White friends from all over the world. I felt blessed that God had made it possible to see all these beautiful people and their lifestyles.

My friend Howard was from Guyana, but he had lived in the United States and was used to comingling. He invited about ten of us to an evening room party. At this party, three of us were Africans, and the rest were Whites and Asians. It was my first real mixed party in a closed room. Since I was not sure what to do, I hid in my small corner. *Would they notice that I was not so friendly?*

A calm female voice said, "Where are you from?"

I turned and saw a middle-aged White woman, British, looking at me.

I took the courage and replied, "From Sierra Leone, West Africa." In those days, in China, you had to partition Africa for your country to be identified quickly. Without adding "West Africa," some smart American was going to ask you if this was near Chicago.

To my surprise, she said "Oh, I have been to Sierra Leone. It's a beautiful country. I love the beaches and the sunshine."

Yes, at last someone in the Far East acknowledged that there are good things in West Africa. I was energized. The rest of the evening went well, and we talked about Freetown's White beaches, and I also talked of my experience in the UK.

The point is that familiarity between people breaks social and racial barriers. The women are usually the first to remove barriers as they encourage their families to be tolerant. They see all as their children, the result of nine months of pain and suffering, leading to the procreation of life. The men, on the other hand, behave differently as society determines. Even those who wouldn't be racist would condone some form of racism to please their peers. Very few Whites have had the guts to stand up to the wave of the times.

⊗ Superiority of The Israelites

The first recorded culture of a human species that claimed superiority were the Israelites. The Israelites' claim to superiority came from the biblical account that the descendants of Abraham and Isaac had been anointed by God Almighty to be a special people. Even though the idea of a special people never meant superior race, it could be seen among Israelites over the years that the continued successes of the Israelites over the races or peoples of the surrounding areas was slowly making them feel superior. The Israelites believe that if anyone puts their absolute trust in the Lord and maker of humanity, Yahweh or Jehovah, and keeps themselves holy through the observance of prescribed laws and relationships with their neighbor, Yahweh blesses them abundantly and lifts them above the others, making them a higher being.

In Deuteronomy 28:1, the Lord promises, "If thou will diligently obey the voice of the Lord your God, to observe carefully all His commandments which I command with you today, that the Lord your God will set you high above all nations of the Earth. And all these blessings shall come upon you and overtake you, because you obey the voice of the Lord."

Israel has held on to several of these promises in the book of Deuteronomy and elsewhere, and this has shaped national policies for generations.

By the 1900s, the Israelites, otherwise known as the Jews, had prospered so much that they became the envy of other nations and peoples. A detailed look into the practices and styles of Israelis shows that they have a focus-driven development and support structures for one another, much like in a clan. Israelis buy and sell Israeli products first and will ensure that there is always an element of recognition of the powers of God in their achievements.

In the Bible, the Israelites overcame the towns of the Hittites, the Jebusites, the Edomites, and the Perizzites (Genesis) on their way to possess the promised land, which was full of milk and honey. While the behavior of the Israelites sometimes seemed unethical and illegal, there was always the factor of repentance for any wrongdoings, and the nation repented through fasting and prayer sessions to the Most High God.

Israel has never sought direct dominance of other nations other than its desire to survive among other nations. No recorded ruler of ancient or modern Israel is seen to be hegemonistic and expansionist for the sake of power and influence. However, Israel continues to develop an agenda of supremacy of its race as a result of "divine appointment" and not by direct military onslaughts.

Interestingly, the Israelites spent most of their sojourn in Europe and the Americas and have had only limited contact with Blacks in Europe and America—but little in Africa. The superiority of the Israeli, therefore, has been manifested among fellow "Whites" of Europe and Palestine. This cannot, in the truest sense, be called racism; it is more of a superiority complex.

Can we conclude that the Israelites are racist toward people with different skin colors? In the incident of the Falasha Jews from Ethiopia, there were signs that some White Israelites attempted to discriminate against them due to color differences. However, an intense period of national debates in the 1970s resulted in the pronunciation by the chief rabbis in 1975 that these Black Jews were also bona fide Jews and worthy of equal treatment under Israeli laws on return.

Rabbis have attempted to preach equality of the various groupings of Jews, irrespective of color, but there are still some who look down on others as being weaker. It seems that as soon as some groupings of humanoids are ostracized and labeled "outsiders," the psychological impact and sometimes the social impact is immense. Productivity drops, and the outlook on the self is affected. It takes a strong will after that for such people to be self-assertive. This is observed in Africa. For hundreds of years, they have been brainwashed to think that the Whiter the skin color, the better the race. Blacks have developed a tendency to immediately give priority and respect to anyone of color who approaches them to the chagrin of the fellow Blacks.

The Falasha Jews need to be given a special developmental package, much as East Europe was propped up at the reunification of the Germans. Billions of dollars were spent because it was all family and one skin color. It becomes an issue with God's chosen people accepting that God made man in his own image and likeness (Genesis 2:26). The Bible never referred to his skin color but to his physical looks, love, kindness, mercy, tenderness, and righteousness. Color was meant to create diversity for humanity, make choices available, and encourage unity in diversity from a truly loving God. Skin color was never meant to be used as a barometer of superior brainpower.

⊗ Superiority of the Romans and Mussolini

The Romans are famous for their militaristic and expansionist approach to development. As Italians and Europeans, the Romans believed that the stronger the nation, the more respect it deserved. There is reason today to confirm that the Romans rejected the supremacy of the Israelites when they invaded and colonized Israel in AD 30–100. The Romans no longer needed to worship the God of the Jews and introduced a new system of religion, which was similar to the Israelite worship but spiritually different. For example, the Israelites worshipped on the Sabbath Day (Saturday), and the Roman worship was centered on the sun god's day.

Under Julius Caesar, Augustus Caesar and Aurelias, Rome developed consistently until the middle of the nineteenth century. The driving philosophy was stoicism. In this ideology, the search for happiness was supreme, and this was satisfied by what man achieved. This was not much different from a materialistic, capitalist world. Therefore, this translated at the state level to a militaristic national agenda.

Could religion play a key part in perpetrating such a situation? No. A semblance of being religious with respect for equality before the law was an accepted way of life. Once someone attained Roman citizenry, his origin became secondary under Roman law. The parallel between equality before the God of all peoples and the equality promised under Roman law made it easy for a quick merging of Roman Mithraism worship with Christianity.

By AD 313, the emperor had succeeded in making Christianity the official religion in Rome while still encouraging the old way of worship. This led to a dilution of the original church doctrines and an eventual breaking away of the Protestant churches in protest.

Because Christianity preaches that all are equal before their maker, you would expect that racism would vanish in the new Rome—and the adopted Christianity. The early preachers of Christianity noted that "God is no respecter of persons" and that God will judge the rich and the poor, the White and the Black, and the good and the wicked using the same standards. Apparently, this has not deterred the Roman rulers and the population from reserving some positions in the church for themselves. For example, in the Roman Catholic Church, there has never been a Black or Asian Pope, and the ratio of Black Cardinals to White Cardinals has no bearing on the ratio of White to Black populations around the world. The head of the Roman Catholic Church has been reserved for White Caucasians!

The Bible claims the equality of all peoples, but the implementers have taken the liberty to interpret it in the Vatican, the seat of Catholic Church power, in a way that suits them. What makes the situation even more twisted is that even when they go through forty days of lockdown and prayers to choose the next head of the church, it always ends up with the same results: a White Caucasian pope from Europe. Has the Holy Spirit never spoken to the assembled cardinals to look at another color of skin as head of the church? I wonder.

Throughout the nineteenth and twentieth centuries, Roman influence, as predicted in the book of Daniel in the Bible, slowly waned. The religious and political power once wielded by the pope and the Roman emperors to appoint and dethrone kings and queens in Europe was finally crushed by Napoleon Bonaparte in the 1890s after the imprisonment of the pope.

A century later, by 1980, Latin, the language of preference of the Roman Catholic Church in the nineteenth and twentieth centuries had been replaced in worship by English and other languages, depending on locality. The church today is a vestige of Greco-Roman power, and Roman influence, politically and religiously, has been eroded.

In the religious realm, more and more countries and peoples of the world have read and understood the Bible and look to a God who is just and who looks on all humanity as his creation and children who are equal in every aspect and can be received equally in his majesty's divine presence through prayer.

Similarly, in the political realm, Rome has few colonial states that look up to it for leadership today. By 1920, Mussolini was leader of Italy and had fostered the Fascist movement. Fascism originated from the Italian word *Fasci*, meaning stronger in unity. They believed in the superiority of the state of Italy over the other states of the world. There was no United Nations Organization then, and the world arena was a free-for-all and the supremacy of the strongest. Fascism developed around a national platform and not so much one of racism, but the partnership of Mussolini and Adolf Hitler introduced a new dimension of racial intolerance and the linking of racism to national politics. We will look at Adolf Hitler's case in the next section. By the end of World War II, in 1949, Fascism had seen its end—and so had Italian and Roman supremacy.

The last two decades in Europe present clearly the downfall of formerly superpower Greco-Roman states. The Greek economy could not sustain itself even after a massive multibillion-dollar bailout by the European Union partners in 2017–2018. Similarly, the legacy of Prime Minister Berlusconi and the system in Italy that ensued showed signs of fragility of the Roman influence globally and left little to envy or to copy.

This position was exacerbated by the poor performance of the entire Italian health system during the COVID-19 pandemic in early 2020. Italy was unprepared, and the rapid spread of the coronavirus ended up causing a lot of fatalities and damage to the economy within six months, further eroding the confidence of smaller nations to look up to the Romans for global leadership.

⊗ The Superiority of the British

Of all the nations comprising the White Caucasian race, the Anglo-Saxons have more tendencies for racism and have traveled the world more than any other race. Those travels have shaped their conception of the people they meet. The Anglo-Saxons refer to that collection of Caucasians of English, Nordic, and Germanic peoples coupled sometimes with the Swedes who have migrated from Northern Europe to the southwest. After settling in England, English became their primary language. The Celts have also inhabited Europe for a long time and combined with the Anglo-Saxons, we have the modern-day European Union. These were a very nomadic, warlike, and colonizing group that has been responsible for the development of colonies of the world and led to the modern industrial revolution.

By the seventeenth century, aided by the East India Company, Britain had colonized the world from North America to Africa and from India to Argentina. France and Spain followed suit and had colonies in Central America, Africa, and Asia. The Germans were a bit controlled and limited the search for colonies to a few countries. Among these European nations, there has always been a competition for superiority and for the largest share. France, Germany, and England fought regional wars and eventually signed truces.

After several wins and defeats, by mutual consent, it became necessary to take the fight out of Europe and over to distant lands where there was a lot of booty to share. The adventures of Marco Polo, Christopher Columbus, Sir Henry the Navigator, and David Livingstone opened the high seas to the rest of Europe in the 1800s.

The British monarchy, the Portuguese, and the Spanish courts were willing to defend the exploits of the brave sailors anywhere they could prove that there was wealth to be acquired. State military apparatuses were sent in defense of their citizen's economic interests.

In 1884–1885, in the famous Balkanization of Africa in Berlin, the brothers and sisters of Europe agreed to carve out Africa and claim rulership. The strongest at the time got the lion's share: Britain and France. The Dutch had also joined in the colonization drive as the Boer Wars intensified in South Africa.

The British expanded their empire and had a colony in every corner of the world, which led to the coining of the phrase: "The sun never sets on the Union Jack." The Union Jack is the famous national flag of Britain. At any given time, as the Earth rotates, the sun must shine on one colony of the Empire in which the flag stood proudly. This was a great success for Britain.

Success can go to the heads of most people, and Britain was no exemption. Over time, the other nations on the island developed. The Irish, Scottish, and Welsh joined the brigade of cavaliers leaving the island for far and distant wars to establish the authority of the queen.

As long as there was victory for all, the four nations of the Island (England, Wales, Scotland, and Ireland) lived in cohabitation. The smaller of them enjoyed the power and fame that came with the success of the United Kingdom. There was no need for a breakup.

All were British, and all claimed superiority over the peoples in the colonies. "Why not call ourselves Great Britain?" The White people of this small island had succeeded in dominating world politics through cunning, hard work, and a vision to become superior to the others. The English language became richer, and it became the language of preference in business and international politics.

In the largest colony, the Americas, the Irish and the British dominated trade and power. With the support of the queen back in England, they were able to overcome the French and the Germans and make America an English colony. Soon, the farms in the newly evolving colony of the United States needed labor. Easily available, cheap labor could be found in the colony, including White persons and lower-class Indo-Chinese.

They soon discovered another race of stronger, hard-muscled people living in a not-too-distant land. Tales of Africa had reached Europe earlier, and adventurous sailors soon thought of the trade in human slaves as a quick moneymaking venture.

The word "slave" gets its origin from the Slavs in northeastern Europe. The Slavs had been the source of cheap labor for generations in Europe, and the English connotation of the word became *slave*. The slave was not only a cheap form of labor; it was a lower standard of humankind. Several rights that we today refer to as human rights were lost to these people. They lost the freedom of movement, the freedom of conscience, and the freedom to even own property. Slaves were molested, beaten, and powerless in a court of law. Slavery continued for more than four hundred years between Africa and Europe and the United States. I will not dwell too much on this. From the racial perspective, the end result is an institutionalized system of looking down on people of Black descent and ancestry.

In the colonies of Britain or France, the Blacks and Chinese had respect from the Whites since they were used to completing the axes of power. The Whites could not succeed in Africa or China without local support. They would be killed and outnumbered in any uprising. Therefore, the British had to use key locals.

The French adopted a system of assimilation, and the British adopted a system of divide and rule. In the French system, the locals who performed well, educated themselves, and adopted French lifestyles were considered equals to a limited extent. This system of assimilation was firmly established and saw such persons like Leopold Sedar Senghor and Felix Houphouet-Boigny becoming representatives in the French National Assembly in the 1950s and 1960s.

The British, on the other hand, used the principle of divide and rule by giving privileges to a select few. They used these to govern at the lower levels while they remained at the higher level as governors. In both cases, however, the success of White rule involved the use of the Blacks and Chinese people and the elites of society to establish colonial rule.

Sometimes, the association of Whites and Blacks did not go well. In the Hut Tax War in Sierra Leone in 1898, the Blacks, headed by a local chief and warrior, Bai Bureh, fought against the British as they refused to pay newly imposed hut taxes. Attempts to convince the locals to pay for government services were seen as incorrect and were rejected. Bai Bureh and his cohorts lost, were arrested, and were sent to exile, but it showed that there was a determination to maintain self-rule and be seen as resisting imperialism.

In another incident of slaves being transported to the Americas in 1839, a young, strong, and proud Black slave resisted the White captives. Sengeh Pieh (Joseph Cinque), a Sierra Leonean, and 52 others on board did not believe the captain and his team had the right to enslave them. They organized, fought, and won a battle on the Amistad ship near the coast of Cuba and took the crew captive. This shows that given certain conditions, Blacks can be superior to their White counterparts. In the courts of the United States at the time, slavery was in the process of being abolished—and they were given a fair trial. Though found guilty, Sengeh Pieh and his colleagues were pardoned and released as free persons. We will look at these instances much more later.

The United States, England, and Spain have always had people with humanitarian and sympathetic hearts for their fellow human beings. William Wilberforce (1759-1830, Granville Sharpe (1735-1813), and others fought hard for the emancipation of slaves. On March 2, 1807, the United States Congress approved a bill to bring to an end slavery. Though the act included fines of up to two thousand dollars for anyone found guilty of the trade, the Whites—in their rebellion against legal systems—found ways to perpetrate this inhuman trade. Ships were stopped but not fined sufficiently large enough sums to discourage them. Once paid off, the fines were not recorded cumulatively and were soon forgotten. This encouraged the sailors to continue to smuggle slaves despite the prohibition of the importation of slaves into the United States.

It wasn't until fifty years later, in 1859, when the last slaves were brought into the United States through the port of Mobile, Alabama. The African Americans started a new journey with their countrymen. By law, these Africans were now Americans in the New World—and equal in rights to the earlier settlers. In principle, the common Whites did not see it so. Why the difference in opinion between the lawmakers and the exploiters? In China today, we see a similar occurrence as a richer class emerges. Must the Black have to be maltreated by all other races each time there is wealth and booty to snatch? What is the crime committed by being born Black? Why, in all of this, don't the Blacks develop hatred for the other races? On the streets, I hear people say, "Hey, brother" to White, Chinese, and Japanese people and it just feels good.

Sometimes I ask myself, *If I could choose my skin color again, what would I ask my maker, my father, and my mother to give me?* The answer comes again and again that I am not the chooser of my skin color and that I am pleased being Black. Being Black may mean I do not have all the opportunities some other people have, but I also will not live among a people who for several millennia have struggled with understanding the simple teachings of one of my mentors: Jesus Christ. This teacher taught that all are equal before the maker and that the God preached by Jesus is no respecter of personalities. Your race, age, social status, and ethnicity are all of one creation. You were created to have diversity and love for differences. Some people love chrysanthemums, some roses, or sunflowers, but they are all beautiful—and they all make the garden a wonderful place to be. I live on a continent where the sun shines bright each day, and there are countless varieties of flowers, fruits, fauna, lovely sand beaches, and a clean natural environment. And I just love being part of it all. I cannot be bothered with one flower having a different color from the ones I like or weeds growing in different forms in my garden. Some weeds drive away snakes. Some flowers have little smell.

European success around the world perpetrated the thought of White supremacy. The Indians in Asia could not resist the firepower of the British. Even the oldest civilization of the Raj could not resist enthusiastic Britons fueled by scientific breakthroughs and the industrial revolution. In South Africa, apartheid was introduced by the Dutch, and the Blacks lost their leadership at the country's helm.

⊗ Slavery in the Middle East and Medieval Europe

Slavery did not commence as a racist institution; it was more of an economic one. In all regions of the world, slavery has been a major part of the history of the peoples. In biblical records of the lands around Israel and in Israel itself, slaves were earned, traded, and kept as part of a family's assets. Slaves were acquired through lack of payments of debts, war booty, or kidnappings by bandits.

In Africa, parents who could not pay for their obligations and debts would sometimes hand over their children as slaves to redeem themselves. Some of these transactions were irreversible, and others were time-bound.

In the seventeenth and eighteenth centuries, the Middle East trade in slaves flourished and included both Whites and Blacks. In Europe, the Portugese were the first to reach Africa on slavery business until action was taken to stop Christian slave trading by passing laws prohibiting the sale of Christian slaves to non-Christians. This changed the dynamics, and then Christian slaves were sold to only Christians, which was eventually completely banned.

However, as discoveries were made of more lands in Africa, crossing over from the Sahara Desert or from sailing the Atlantic and Indian Oceans, more Blacks were introduced into the slave trade by direct purchases rather than debt-recovery measures. Guns, gunpowder, mirrors, and fine clothing were used as mediums of exchange with the quantity varying, depending on the build for men and the desirability for women. These were no longer based on moral issues and debt repayment; it was plain business with the objective of making a profit.

The Arabs traveled from the Middle East and transported African slaves back to the Middle East. When there were mixed-color slaves, the White slave attracted more value than the Black slave out of sympathy for their kin. The White slave dealer became conscious that the sale of humans was only bad when faced with a multiracial choice and the cost to purchase the slave. It was purely business.

In time, it became cheaper to have Black slaves for menial and farm work and the White slaves for more domestic and home care work. The norm began to be established for inferiority of the Blacks, even among slaves. The Black leaders were accomplices in selling their brothers and sisters to the highest bidder, not knowing that this undermined the race values that once existed that all men were made equal.

Slavery had been abolished by the federal government in the United States, but different states continued to enact laws that perpetrated the practice and made the Blacks still inferior. Some forced freed slaves to have only menial or low-paying jobs. Some pay was so low that the females preferred to stay home and be caregivers than to go work for peanuts.

The emancipated Blacks were not so entrepreneurial, and credit facilities were not made available to develop small-scale artisanal businesses. Banks could not give loans to Blacks without several levels of guarantee requirements. This was a barrier to progress and self-emancipation.

⊗ The Ideology of the Ku Klux Klan and American White Supremacy

Soon after the abolition of slavery in the United States, the Whites who could not accept the loss of such huge amounts of cheap labor passed many laws to limit the rapid growth of cost of labor among the freed slaves. Meanwhile, another set of pro-Whites decided to organize themselves in an organization that would continue the fight underground to perpetrate the ideology of supremacy of the Whites. Interestingly, most of these Whites were Christian. They must have had childhood education in Sabbath schools and in Sunday schools that all men were created equal and we must love the other as we love ourselves. However, these teachings do not seem to have been well received in the minds of these men and women. Over generations, it must have come to be accepted that among Christians, some will be treated by God better than others when they reach heaven because of the skin color God gave them or because they never understood the teachings and only pretended to be Christians.

Mahatma Gandhi said that he loved Christ and his teachings but did not love purported Christians who only went to church for the formalities and never truly loved God and his creations. They never agreed that God should have created other humans than White-skinned people and that God was wrong to allow Whites and Blacks to share the same lands and buildings.

General Nathan Bedford Forrest was one such Christian. In 1866, he founded the Ku Klux Klan with the expressed objective of perpetrating White supremacy, contrary to law and contrary to the beliefs of Christianity to which he claimed to belong. His organization grew in the United States and was responsible for thousands of lynchings of both Blacks and Whites within forty years of its establishment. Yes, Whites as well. Any White man who sympathized with the Blacks and supported Blacks in politics, business, or the fight for freedom was a target and could be threatened, blackmailed, or even lynched. The organization burnt down churches and schools that belonged to Blacks or were promoting rapid progress of many Blacks. Across the American South, many were threatened and attacked.

President Ulysses S. Grant was determined to have racial equality. He passed the Ku Klux Klan Act of 1871 to stifle the organization and stop racial violence, but more Whites joined the movement. At its peak, the KKK reached four million members—and millions more sympathizers. It was a formidable force.

The population of Black Americans in those days was less than ten million, and you can imagine what damage an army of hate-driven people can achieve. The unseen hand of the KKK could wreck any chances of getting a good job, a promotion, a successful business, and even a good reputation in just about any part of the English-speaking world. They were not much different from the modern-day Freemasons who advocate for their members irrespective of the character.

What was the reason for all these actions by the KKK? To prevent the man with Black skin from occupying high office and making judgment over any White-skinned person.

The KKK movement was different from racism in other countries. In the United States, the Whites were not from the same country or the same religion. They were from different parts of Europe—with different cultures—but they were motivated by hate for the Blacks and for those who truly believed in human rights and the equality of the races.

While some Whites came from non-English-speaking or non-Spanish-speaking countries, they were still treated as Americans. The accents of some of these stand out a mile away, and the defensive stance is to speak little in public gatherings so that their true identities are not revealed. Instead of accepting that they were all immigrants anyway, they preferred to join the KKK movement and other anti-Black and anti-Semitic movements to suppress the rights of others, including freed slaves, so that they thought they could get better.

Some racism is economic in nature, and some is just fanatism and copycat behavior with no justification. In all these cases, the movement looked real but was like a bubble that will burst—no matter how many centuries it takes.

For Blacks to be accepted, they needed to have a certain disposition. Marcus Garvey Jr. was an intelligent African American who studied the White man enough to know that behaving in some ways would make them leave you in peace and allow you to develop your skills. "Saying 'Yes, sir, master' does not remove the pants off you" is a popular parable in English West Africa.

In World War I, several Blacks saved the lives of their White countrymen, but as soon as they returned home, those acts of goodwill were forgotten. Skin color crowded memories. Benefits due to war veterans were delayed or denied in full. Was not the fight for the same country?

The KKK still remains an underground force that cannot understand that Blacks were meant to populate the United States and stay there to help build the continent to the level it has achieved today. Some of those Whites died miserably, and some were never recognized as heroes for their heinous crimes, but their children seem to be happy to be underground and nurturing their hatred in twenty-first century America.

⊗ The Superiority of Adolf Hitler's Aryan Race, Nazism, and Quasi German Supremacy

As Fascism was taking over in Italy, Prime Minister Benito Mussolini and his colleagues succeeded in energizing Italians into strong nationalistic fervor. In Germany, Adolf Hitler, a decorated military officer, had been the spy on the *Deutsche Arbeiter partei* (DAP).

In 1920, he formally joined them after being convinced of their nationalistic and anti-socialist ideologies.

By 1921, Hitler was made chairman of the renamed party, *Nationalsozialistische Deutsche Arbeiter partei.* NSDAP was shortened to the Nazi Party. The Nazis grew rapidly in Germany. Amid the collapse of stock markets in 1929 and the global depression that followed, the Nazis performed well at economics and elections. They soon won seats in the national elections, and Hitler was made chancellor in 1933. Within two years, he created the new title of *Fuhrer,* the Supreme Leader.

The Nazis saw nationalism and the establishment of a super race of people with no mixed blood as a primary goal of the state. This stance included the elimination of Jews in the national economics as a key political ideology and the expunging of persons of mixed blood from public office.

Brainwashed with Hitler's super Aryan race teachings, Germans were wary of miscegenation. Miscegenation was the mixing of races through inter-marriages, cohabitation, and procreation that leads to a perceived impurity of one of the races. The Aryan race of Germanic people should not be polluted. This was a major blunder in German politics, and the country has ever since grappled with how to remove this stain from its history.

Adolf Hitler and his wife, Eva, died a questionable but miserable death by suicide in 1945. Hitler could not stand losing to other non-Aryan armies and was determined to take his own life rather than be captured and learn the hard lesson that no one man or race is superior to others in this world. After Hitler's death, racism continued, and it is still seen in major incidents.

Racism and violence against the Jews was a very unique form of racism, and it led to the Holocaust in which the Nazis eliminated more than six million Jews in several concentration camps. This was one of the extreme forms of racism and genocide ever experienced in the world. It was racism of Whites against "Whites." Depending on which definition you took, the Brazilians would see the Jews as White, but the Germans of Hitler's group did not.

In 1903 and 1908, the German Empire was being established, copying the likes of Spain, Portugal, Britain, and France. As part of this imperialistic expansion, they waged war on the locals and practiced racism in Namibia. This ended in the genocide of the *Ovaherero*, the Nama, and the San people in what was then German South West Africa. Initially the Germans denied the allegations, but the investigations of the United Nations into the incidents eventually produced the Whitaker Report in 1985, which classified them as genocide. During this genocide, the heads of thousands of Blacks were cut off and taken to Germany as proof of "superiority." The Hottentots and the Venus Hottentot concepts showed Black features as being "inferior," and they were the laughingstock of elite German society.

Adolf Hitler's Germany extended Jewish anti-Semitism to Black racism. Theodore Michael, an Afro German, wrote *Black German*. He was sometimes confused about German racism. If a Black joined the army and fought on the German side, he was accepted as a friend and partner, but he was immediately discriminated against if he behaved otherwise. Racism in Germany has been fluid, and it was worst meted out against Jews. The Nazis and the Aryan race concept meant that large parts of Germany participated in the discrimination and genocide of peoples of other colors. However, the small proportion that did not saved the national image.

My sister-in-law lives in the United States, but she dates a young German doctor who practices in West Africa. For more than twenty years, this doctor has been residing in Ghana, Sierra Leone, and recently in Conakry, Guinea. He spends a fortune on plane tickets and staying at hotels in different countries to follow the love he has for this Black beauty.

It all started when German diplomats organized parties for their rotating expats. These expats come to Africa, and over the course of their stays, they make friends with the locals. Naturally, the young African girls have heard of Adolf Hitler, the Nazis, and their racist practices, and they instinctively avoid the Germans as much as possible. However, the younger Germans do not want to associate with 1940s German history and try very hard to avoid this stigma. They are overfriendly, laugh a lot, and go to extreme corners and villages, living with the people, eating their foods, and sleeping in the same conditions as their friends. This new approach to living has won over my beautiful sister-in-law and many other women. There are now more intermarriages with Germans than previously known.

⊗ The Superiority of the Dutch in South Africa's Apartheid

The most recent case of state-sponsored White supremacy ended on African soil in 1990 when Nelson Mandela won the general elections and became South Africa's first Black president. Though this ended White rule, it has not completely eliminated the thoughts of White supremacy.

Southern Africa has been experiencing an organized development dating back as far as the 1200s when the kingdom of Great Zimbabwe was established by the Shona people with a king. The economy relied on livestock, farming, and mining to advance their development. Through trades with the peoples of South Africa to the south and the extremes of Egypt in the north, the people of Great Zimbabwe established a royal court and advanced architecture, building ten-meter-high structures like the conical tower and two- and three-story buildings. In those days, technology was similar to Europe or even better. Much like the Qing Dynasty and the Great Wall of China, the kingdom is reported to have built walls around the settlements, and the residents lived in small cities that could have had populations of up to twenty thousand inhabitants.

Leonard Thompson is the author of the *History of South Africa*. Though the Republic of South Africa today is a complex mix of cultures and races of Blacks, British, Afrikaans, and Indians, it all started with a country that was once all Black Africans. Since 1000 BC, there is evidence that other Black people moved into the region, and there was migration from as far as the Horn of Africa, Ethiopia, Somalia, and the Cape of Africa. Since that time, the major tribes—the Bantu, the Xhosa, the Sans, and the Zulus—have made South Africa home.

By AD 700, trade with the Arabs had commenced. Whites started having an interest in the country and the Southern region. From Zanzibar, where the Arabs settled, to Nairobi and Cape Town, the sheer beauty and pristine environment—with its beautiful beaches and friendly atmosphere—was a small heaven on Earth.

The Portuguese took an affirmative stance. Bartholomew Diaz sailed around the cape in 1480, further discovering the beauty of the country. The race for control of the country had begun. As usual, the natives were unsuspecting and assumed this was another of their kind coming to enjoy nature, but they were wrong. The kings of the Zulu, the Xhosa, and the Sans could not withstand what happened in the following two hundred years. The Dutch arrived and forcibly settled down, only to be dislodged temporarily by the British. This was followed by the Boers winning the next war.

Life in South Africa would never be the same again. Diamonds that used to be jewelry for royalty were now mined in large amounts and smuggled out of the country without much royalty paid to the landowners. In the view of the Europeans, all was up for grabs.

It became worse toward the end of the nineteenth century when gold was discovered in Cape Town. This led to a war between the British and the Dutch. The British overseas army was stronger and took over again, establishing South Africa as a Crown colony of the British Empire!

Britain granted independence to South Africa in 1912, and soon after that, the Whites on the ground started showing their true ambitions. They passed the law banning the natives of the land from gaining access to land (in their own country!), and the rest is history.

By 1949, the Afrikaans Party won the elections and promulgated a new racist segregationist regime called apartheid with laws that prohibited Blacks and Whites from attending the same schools, the same beaches, or the same transportation. This was déjà vu for the United States. The cousins of the White Europeans operating in the United States had arrived in South Africa.

Skin color has always been an issue for Europeans. While scientific evidence shows all humans have two eyes, two ears, two legs, and the same number of muscles, bones, nerves, and brain size, these Europeans only saw the superficial look of humanity. They failed to see the beauty in diversity and only saw opportunities to extort. They failed to see humility and only saw the wealth of the humble people, and they grew jealous and greedy. Why had the maker not placed them in this garden of gold and diamonds and made them see snow for six months per year? Little did they know that if only they had looked farther, there was gold, coal, oil, and gas below those snowcapped mountains. Why maltreat other humans for the things that were in their backyards?

In South Africa, the children of generations of Blacks watching the Whites on this stage performing injustice, greed, and hatred decided it was time to stop the carnival. The Native African Council had been representing Black interests but was replaced by the African National Congress (ANC).

The ANC was more sophisticated and dedicated to the cause of racial equality, and they were endowed with more educated members like Steve Biko and a son of one of the chiefs, Nelson Mandela, and his colleagues. They took up the challenge of fighting for the kids in Soweto, for the Asians in Johannesburg, and for the land their forefathers left behind for them. In short, there had to be equality of the races if they were all going to have their children enjoy a prosperous South Africa.

Nelson Mandela was so vocal that in 1962, he was arrested and sentenced to life imprisonment. One would have thought that was the end, but energized by unseen hands, young Nelson accepted prison life and continued his operations from prison. His actions and protests gained the attention of the international community, and Britain, the United States, and the African Union championed a change of regime in South Africa.

Racist Pieter W. Botha was replaced with Frederik De Klerk as president. President De Klerk had a lot of respect for the now old man, Nelson Mandela. After twenty-seven years in prison on Robin Island in South Africa, breaking stones that probably no one used to build houses or fences but only to punish someone for thinking of wanting to be equal to the Whites, all they could see in this tall, crouching Mandela was admiration. These two leaders agreed to build a new South Africa, causing both to win the Nobel Peace Prize in 1991. Apartheid was scrapped, and the rights of Blacks were restored.

Given equal rights to vote, modern democracy gives victory to the majority. The ANC won the elections of 1991, and Blacks ruled South Africa again. Nelson Mandela became the first Black president of the country. In the euphoria that followed, the Africans expected immediate changes in their economic status because of a Black president.

In the United States, many people expected things would be righted overnight with Barack Obama as the first Black president. They forget that Blacks had been suppressed for four hundred years by their White friends, brothers, and sisters all in the name of development. How can so much lagging behind be restored in ten years? Development could have happened anyway without racism. For example, in the purely homogenous nonracial countries of Sweden, Norway, and pre-World War II Japan, where all are treated equally except for economic status, had development not been achieved without racism and exploitation of other races? The racist Whites need to ponder and answer these questions.

Nelson Mandela is to be remembered as a statesman. He stepped down in 1992—not even two years after ascending to the presidency. His mission had been completed. He needed to share the story around the world—a story of love for his people and country and how hatred of some Whites for Blacks and Colored people could be overturned by sustained belief in the fundamental rights of equality of all peoples as agreed at the United Nations and as enshrined in the Bible and Quran for all humanity.

While racism is still practiced by Whites in South Africa, life for many Blacks and Coloreds is improving. Even without cheap forced labor, there are many Black millionaires among the once poor and oppressed—gained through hard work and proper business-management skills.

The above sections prove that racism, racial supremacy, and ultra-rightist ideologies do not last forever and are not necessary for development. From Babylon to Rome, from South Africa to Tunisia, equality will be established.

Generations of Whites have tried to suppress their fellow humans and lived off the sweat of these hundreds of millions, but in the end, it has been the same result: they were toppled and replaced by a more egalitarian system, whether through communism, outright capitalism, or so-called democracies.

Racism will end, but humans will continue to need each other—and humanity will progressively become mixed. In the end, given equal opportunities, all humanity can be at their best. The apple is big, and everyone can have a share without being envious of the other's cut.

⊗ The Neutrality of the Sierra Leoneans and West Africans in General

While I was growing up in Sierra Leone, there were no major issues with race. As early as the 1900s, my grandfather from my mother's side was a paramount chief, the highest ruler in a chiefdom. Chief Samura Fombo I was a fighter from the Kambia District in the Northern Province. The family settled in the Sanda Loko chiefdom in today's Karene District. As a chief, his court was always full of people from different chiefdoms and regions paying homage. As part of the tradition of the chiefdoms, all visitors are expected to pay homage to the reigning paramount chief before they can be allowed to settle in. This custom had both security implications as well as economic ones.

From a security standpoint, it ensured that his chiefdom was assured of its safety through this system of initial vetting. The visitor was to recount his origin, his relatives, and his destination. Only when all of these were satisfactorily answered was the permission to dwell given. These rules applied to all—irrespective of skin color or origin. From an economic standpoint, it meant that the paramount chief was the first to get wind of any new developments and business opportunities in his chiefdom.

All visitors to my grandfather's house were treated equally. In fact, in general, visitors were more welcome than natives at the chief's house. These traditions have been passed down through the ages, and to this day, when we have more traveling going on around the world, West Africans see all people as the same and must be treated equal before the law.

Many foreign races have taken advantage of this goodwill, signed unfair concessions, exploited the region's natural resources, made slaves of them, and looked down on these people in their reduced economic state. Should the African let this situation continue? When will this disadvantageous open-door policy stop? The difference in development as a result of this simplistic outlook has reached mammoth proportions, and it might not be possible to reverse some of the losses.

CHAPTER FOUR

Population Analysis of the Races

LONG BEFORE THE CONCEPT OF DEMOCRACY SET IN, THE PRINCIPLE of "two heads are better than one" already existed. In the Bible book of Ecclesiastes 4:9, this idiom was first quoted by the wise old King Solomon.

Greek and modern democracy have come to teach the rule of the majority. It is possible that an understanding of world population dynamics can help us understand the institution of racism in new ways in which the majority have been lording it over the others. And as this dynamic evolved, a new relationship was developing.

The world's population has been recorded since the 1500s, and this can help us understand demographics and human growth trends. According to world population figures of the United Nations, Blacks made up close to 14 percent of world population in those early days while Whites were 33 percent. This was almost double that of the Blacks, and this was a major advantage in terms of war and military personnel. It was not surprising that Whites could easily win wars against their Black counterparts with gunpowder technology borrowed from the Chinese.

The Chinese and Indians had always been very populous. They constituted 49 percent of world population then. Though the Asians did not travel far then, their sheer population created advantages or should we say opportunities in business and economics?

With a strong centralized government during the Ming and Qin Dynasties, China was able to have advanced technologies that the Europeans envied and very quickly copied. These included gunpowder, paper, suspension bridges, money, and silk.

From the look of things, Asia was advanced, second only to Africa in Egypt, Timbuctoo and Zimbabwe. Hispanics only made up 5–7 percent of the world's population.

Four hundred years later, in 1900, the figures had changed dramatically. A combination of factors had affected the population of Whites, Blacks, and Hispanics—but not Asians. Slavery had a major impact on Blacks during this period. The Black population dropped to 9 percent, the White population dropped to 30 percent, and the Hispanic population dropped to around 6 percent. On the contrary, the Asian and Indo-Chinese populations saw a major jump of more than 8 percent.

In 1800, the world was able to record its first billion people on Earth. It had taken the world thousands of years to reach that point. The world was a fairly racially tolerant one with economics driving the supremacy of the nations and less of the skin color. Without looking closely at the underlying factors, there was a risk of creating a nexus between skin color and economic growth. Africa, home to the world's Blacks, is seen as poor, and Europe and the Americas, which are mostly White, are seen as rich. This school of thought has been ongoing for too long and is known as the *geography hypothesis*.

By 1930, the world's population had doubled—after only 130 years. Again, the Indo-Chinese population was the major cause of the rapid population growth. Why was the population rising so fast during a period when the rest of the world's population was dwindling? Some attribute this to a period of peace and economic growth and fewer controls on family size.

Figure 2 below shows the population trends of the races over the past five hundred years and the projected figures for the next 120 years. In the hundred years before 2010, the world population continued to grow and attained 7.8 billion inhabitants. It had taken the world only eighty years to rise by four billion. Slavery had almost ended, and the Black population was beginning to recover.

The population of the world and every race is continuously growing, but the growth patterns are different. For Blacks, it reached 16 percent of world population, Indo-Chinese populations continued to grow to 62 percent, and White populations dropped to 19 percent. The Hispanic population rebounded and reached 9 percent. The number of Whites and Blacks around the world in 2020 was almost equal at one billion each. Further studies and projections show that, by 2030, there will be more Blacks on Earth than Whites.

According to the Brookings Institute, a major think tank in the United States, Whites will become a minority (less than 50 percent) of the American population by 2045. Whites will make up 49.7 percent of the population against 13.1 percent for Blacks, 24.6 percent for Hispanics, 7.9 percent for Asians, and 3.8 percent for multiracial populations. This means there will be more non-White people in the United States and this could have impact both on socioeconomic trends and political voting patterns.

Nations have maintained about 4 percent of their populations for military purposes. In Europe, there is an aging population generally, and minorities are gaining more rights through the universal voting franchise of one man, one vote. If it came to the physical numbers, the combined armies of the world would see larger non-White armies than White armies. Also, the combined populations of Asians and Blacks make Whites a minority in the world.

More non-White persons can support global peace missions in

a world that is becoming increasingly hostile. Europe, the United States, and Canada are going to need more minorities to run operations worldwide. Europe is closing its doors to full-fledged citizenship for non-Whites in a show of reverse colonialism, but the Germans need more people—and so do the Swedes and Norwegians.

So, White man, how much longer do you think you can remain superior? The clock is ticking. Can race inequality continue to be a winning strategy for Whites?

⊗ The United Nations and Equality of Nations and Peoples

Voting rights at the United Nations are based on the principle of equality of nations and peoples. The General Assembly uses one country, one vote on major issues. But due to covert racism, the major decisions of the UN are still influenced by the White man. Notwithstanding this, among the 193 member states and institutions, at least sixty-nine countries are predominantly negro-race member states, thirty-four are predominantly White, and twenty-two are Indo-Chinese. All it takes is a coalition of non-White votes for the plans and wishes of the White supremacy ideologies to be overcome and defeated in the UN.

However, it's not so simple. The hard reality is that the White-dominated nations are the richest and contribute the most to the UN, making their lobbying power real by linking aid to support of their agendas at the UN. The UN is committed in policy to anti-racial discrimination acts in all its forms. In consideration of the Charter of the United Nations establishment, the Universal Declaration of Human Rights states that all humans are created equal and must be treated so.

In consideration of the stance of the United Nations in bringing colonialism to an end, the UN passed the Convention on the Elimination of All Forms of Racial Discrimination (CERD) in

1965. The UN CERD has hopes that we will get there if we will see a public call for equality. Individuals may still cherish their hopes of being seen as superior to others—even if for just the short life span they have on Earth.

In the fifty-five years since the CERD convention, member states should have all accepted equality of peoples and races. Eighty-eight member countries have signed this convention, and almost all 193 members have ratified it. Some members have expressed reservations on certain clauses with regard to the treatment of racism or mentioned real reasons for "not wanting interference in their internal affairs."

The United States, China, and some Caribbean countries have reservations relative to their internal laws, and this shows the difficulty of converging on key issues of world development and common humanity. Some countries do not recognize the clause that all members in a dispute have to agree before it is forwarded to the International Court of Justice in The Hague as the court of jurisdiction.

The United Nations is still dominated by the Group of Five Security Council members with three of them—the United Kingdom, France, and Russia being White—and one being Indo-Chinese, China and one multiracial, the United States of America. China has often affiliated with the so-called nonaligned countries, mostly poor and developing countries with majority-Black nations for support, and this has paid off very well. We will look at this in the chapter on superpowers and race relations.

As the developing countries have gained more knowledge and acceptance over the decades of the rules of the international diplomatic arena, there have been calls for the most populous continent after Asia to be aptly represented in the United Nations Security Council. This is not only about population issues. The hard reality is there has been a conscious overlooking of the representation of Black people because of the absence of nuclear power in the region.

While the general opinion is that nuclear power is bad for humanity, for Africans it is being used as a criterion for discriminating against 20 percent of the world's population in Africa. Even with these facts, the UN continues to claim that it is a fair institution to all its members. Economics is not the driver—racism is.

The UN has spent the past ten years debating whether Africans are qualified to be permanent members in the UNSC while several notable Blacks, like Kofi Anan, James Jonah, and Boutros Boutros-Ghali, have headed the UN. This touches on the point that while individuals are accepted as equal, superior, and/or capable, the race of Blacks as a whole is still marginalized. This is economic racism at work in the world. At the UN General Assembly in 2021, the President Julius Maada Bio of the small West African nation Sierra Leone thought it was again time to make this call. He called for two permanent seats at the UN Security Council with full veto rights! Why not for a continent with more than one billion people?

I will not delve much more into the Security Council situation because it was set up in a way that any single permanent member, irrespective of its racial bias, cannot dominate the other four members. Therefore, though each member of the council has a veto power, the People's Republic of China and Russia have continuously made it clear that they will not tag along racist pro-White, pro-NATO ideologies.

Communism has, to some extent, tried to close the gap in racial relations and exposed capitalism's racist tendencies. The state votes of the UK, France, and the United States cannot use the council to push a racist agenda. The era of the White man as supremacist is waning. What can they do to make themselves more relevant in a fast-paced world without barriers?

The United Nations Educational, Scientific, and Cultural Organization (UNESCO) has also being involved in raising awareness of race issues since the 1950s. From the outcome of two key international conferences on race, the observations of the scientists were that there has not been enough scientific data to conclude that differences in performances and the rights of persons could be based on race alone. During these debates, of course, there were divergences of view—but not enough to refute the rights of persons to equal treatment around the world.

Ultra-racists like Canadian psychologist J. Philippe Rushton, the author of *Race, Evolution, and Behavior: A Life History Perspective*, have attempted to convince other scientists and psychologists that there is a relationship between race and behavior patterns, that intellectual ability can be tied to race and skin color, and that even sexuality is related to race. However, he forgets that Blacks are not the most populous race in the world. For a long time, Whites and the Indo-Chinese have been more numerous. It was only in the past hundred years that—faced with the possibility of extinction and perpetual minority in the international arena—Blacks started looking at increasing their population and strength.

Still, the rate of growth of Chinese and Indians is unbeatable. The number of Blacks in the world can never match that of the Asians or the rate of growth of their population. Rushton may not have visited Dakar in Senegal or Abuja in Nigeria to see how complex Africans can be. He may not have seen the change of West Africans from the days of coup d'états in the 1960s and 1970s to the present democratic dispensations to understand that there is enough intelligence and self-control among Africans to build economies larger than some European ones. All he saw were the skyscrapers of New York and Ontario as signs of intellect and development.

I often tell my kids and colleagues that even the five-year-old Black child has more intelligence and brainpower than the most advanced supercomputer or robot. It will take many decades before artificial intelligence can overtake natural intelligence. Mature Africans are just as intelligent as the best Caucasians and Indo-Chinese; it's all a matter of environment, priority, and preferences.

Reflections
Where a man's Treasure is that's where his heart is. —Jesus Christ Those who take care of great things also take care of small things. —African proverb When a man's instincts are evil, repentance has a short lease and brief is his gratitude toward those who have done him good. — Khushwant Singh

CHAPTER FIVE

The Pursuit of Superpower Status, Economic Performance, and the Racism Nexus

THE WORLD'S ECONOMY IS GROWING DAILY AT A RATE NEVER before imagined. Every nation's economy seems to have grown bigger over the past fifty years in terms of volume, but national debts also seem to be ballooning as more nations resort to borrowing against a future only imagined in stock markets and government bonds. Several measures have been used to determine the size and success of the productivity of nations, and the most common are gross domestic product (GDP), gross domestic product (by purchasing power parity (PPP)) and balance of trade (BoT).

The GDP measures the aggregate value of all goods and services produced in the country at nominal US dollar value, while the GDP (PPP) measures the same production as the GDP but takes account of the value of the local currency in its national setting. For example, when I was in the United States, I bought a can of soda for $1.29 at a Walmart. This same can of soda in Sierra Leone cost USD 0.55. This means I could have two and half cans of soda in Sierra Leone for the same amount of one can in the United States. Purchasing power parity helps us appreciate the cost of living from country to country and shows why even though developing countries may have low salaries, their living standards can be higher than expected.

The world's economy is dominated by the Group of Twenty (G-20). This is a grouping of nineteen states and the rest of the European Union. According to World Bank and IMF estimates in 2020, together they make up 79 percent of the world's economy; the rest of the world's 173 countries combined only make up the remaining 21 percent of the world's economy. I pondered these facts and thought that even on the world stage, the Pareto ratio seemed to hold; 10 percent of the world's nations produce 90 percent of its output. But the figures speak far beyond this simple analysis of facts.

I am convinced that if people looked at the performances of the world from a racial perspective and not only from an economic one, there would be much more than meets the eye. Doing so makes good reading. There is a strong correlation between the economy of the G-20 and the races in the world. There are hidden racial wars at play, and this needs to be understood. I have been to some of these great nations and seen how the races live among themselves, and I see the Indo-Chinese making massive gains over the other races in economic performance, but they continue to lag behind on social issues that affect global race relations. In the following pages, I will try to explain what I saw under the sun.

The United States, South Africa, and Brazil are heterogeneous, unlike the other nations of the G-20. This means there is no one dominant race to which the aggregate production of the United States or Brazil can be attributed. Caucasians would love to be considered the main cause of the huge outputs of these nations, but considering the fact that the United States has only 49 percent Caucasians, the contributions of the other races making up 51 percent cannot be overlooked. In fact, even though it is through the ownership of the companies that the large riches are attributed, nonetheless, the input to the factors of production in any aggregate output are mostly by the Hispanic, Black, and Indo-Chinese residents of these countries. I have therefore taken the United States, South Africa, and Brazil out as not being outright Caucasian, Black, or Indo-Chinese and combined their outputs as mixed-race economies.

In Figure 4 below, the pie chart shows the share of the world's economy from a racial perspective. We have captured the GDP (PPP) of the world's top twenty economies—and Africa—and done some analysis. We see that of the twenty richest nations, homogeneous Caucasian economies, make up 27 percent of the world's economy, and Indo-Chinese economies make up a whopping 45 percent. The United States and Brazil are among the largest economies, but they are considered mixed-race economies because of the composition of the different races. When combined, they make up 22 percent of the global economy.

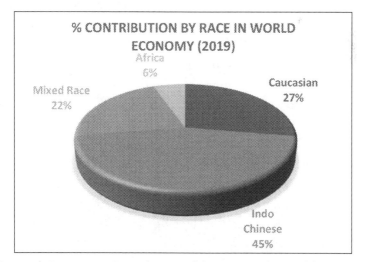

Figure 4: Percentage Contribution of the races to the World's Economy (2019) Source : IMF Statistics, Analysis and Image by Author

Pure Black economies of Africa and some in the Caribbean make up only 6 percent of the global riches annually, but they are growing at a very fast rate. No single African economy reached a trillion dollars.

What all this means is that firstly, the Indo-Chinese race is leading the world economy and production. Secondly, while pure White economies are declining relatively, Black and Indo-Chinese economies are improving. Thirdly, the giant pure Black economy of Nigeria is better than many pure White or pure Asian economies from a GDP perspective—but the Black countries of the world continue to have a poor performance economically.

In today's materialistic world, money and finance are the key to everything. The poor are marginalized and are hardly heard in the UN or on the global stage. This leads to poor social status and discrimination. The pursuit of superpower status among nations has created a de facto racial inequality status that cannot be resolved without concrete actions by the UN Security Council. While the Convention on the Debarment of Racial Discrimination is a potent UN tool, there are no affirmative actions signed into conventions to reverse the effects of slavery or discrimination for four hundred years against Blacks, which forced Africa's backwardness. It does not appeal to the Whites who control the UN, and it does not appeal to the Asians who avoid the topic because they stand to gain from the status quo as they pursue the gradual dominance of the Whites and consequently the Blacks, a minority in the world. In fact, it would seem the Indo-Chinese are better at exploiting the Blacks, taking immediately after the colonialism of the Caucasians.

With sixty years of independence, Nigeria, a pure Black economy, has leveraged its natural resources and human capital to become the largest economy in Africa. Overlooking the size of the population for a while, we observe annual growth that is commendable. Botswana, Rwanda, Ghana, and other all pure Black economies have shown that given the chance and the free will, Africa can make it.

If Africa had enjoyed uninterrupted and free access to the world economy over the past four hundred years and had been treated as equals in world politics and world trade—with fair prices and access to credit facilities—the situation would have been different. Instead, Europe and the rest of the world have established strong and resilient market systems that it will take at least some time to catch up.

Should Blacks be allowed to compete freely as equals? Yes! Africans deserve to trade their natural resources and human capital at good prices to spur on their economies. If this inequality continues, the Caucasians and Indo-Chinese should have some element of remorse for treating fellow humans in such a harsh and negligent manner. Of course, not all humans are religious and God-fearing. I found out this truth under the sun. This means that Blacks have to rise to the challenge and reestablish their worth on the world stage.

As already raised earlier, this analysis can get complex when we look at GDP per capita and the Gini coefficient. The Gini coefficient measures the disparity between income groups in a country, but it can also be used to determine inequality between races in an economy or across economies. This coefficient was developed by Corrado Gini, an Italian statistician. For a country of perfect equality, the Gini coefficient would be 1(one), and for those with imperfect inequality, the coefficient would be zero. The figure registered for the world was 0.5 in 1820. In those years, it was assumed that a perfect world existed—and people were more tolerant of each other. The facts changed over the years, and by the turn of the century, disparity increased. It has been increasing since World War I (1917).

Today, according to the World Bank's Christoph Lakner and others, the world's Gini coefficient was around 0.705 in 2008, and in the United States, it was 0.45. This shows there is much disparity in the world's incomes. The twenty richest nations are getting even richer as they continue to pursue policies that do not attempt to reduce these disparities and force poorer nations to be even poorer. The brunt of this falls on Black Africans who were left out of major deals and technological advances for more than four hundred years. It is amazing that more and more Africans and Asians can afford to buy luxury cars and large mansions and even eat complete meals. Thanks to the work of the United Nations, awareness is settling in, albeit slowly. Thanks to changes in national policies, the world is less hungry.

Economist Francois Bourguignon has done a lot of research on race and economic performance. According to Bourguignon, in a report from 2002, the disparity between nations explains the disparity between economies of the world. What he did not say was that the practice of racial supremacy was at the core of the disparity.

The box below includes an excerpt from a nineteenth-century speech by Lord Macauley that proposed a strategy to brainwash the colonies and install British values or else fail in their mission of hegemonism and supremacy.

I have traveled the length and breadth of India, and I have not seen one person who is a beggar, who is a thief, such wealth I have seen in this country, such high moral values, people of such caliber that I do not think we would ever conquer this country, except we break the very backbone of this nation, which is her spiritual and cultural heritage. I therefore propose that we replace her old and ancient education system, her culture. For if the Indians think that all that is foreign and English is good and greater than their own, they will lose their self-esteem, their native culture, and they will become what we want them, a truly dominated nation.

—Lord Macauley's Address to British Parliament, Feb 2, 1835, on India and Cultural Dominance

---

⊗ The Theory of Climate-Influenced Culture

In the search for survival in cold climates, the principle of survival of the fittest comes into play. Nordic climates are much harsher than tropical regions where food is in abundance all year round and the need for clothing to protect against inclement weather of various forms is lesser. From my experience in the cold winter winds of Siberia, I soon acknowledged that Caucasians and others in the caucuses and Upper Indo-Chinese of Japan have been forced by nature to think and work harder than their tropical counterparts in order to survive.

In this pursuit of self-preservation, internal instincts have been honed over thousands of years to make the people more aggressive, demanding, and less emotional than their counterparts in Africa and Lower Asia. For example, while death from natural causes can be difficult in the family, it is soon forgotten, and life carries on its course among these cold-surviving races.

Over time, certain personalities with stronger will created the class of lords, the samurai, and the bourgeoisie, and they established power and economic blocs within national borders. As experienced in Roman and other nation's histories, family wealth and aggressive developments transformed to national aggregate wealth, and then international competition between the richer nations was born. Initially, racism was not at the core of international competitions. Most of humanity accepted equality as a God-given right.

However, with the discovery of Blacks in Africa and Indo-Chinese in the 1600s in environments of much friendlier dispositions and natural wealth, the aggressive character in the Caucasian and Upper Indo-Chinese (Aryan) was stimulated once again. This cycle of events led to the race for colonialism, hegemonism, and an industrial need for natural resources.

As Europe expanded, the exploitation of Africa and Asia increased. The first class of nations with superpower status was declared in the 1950s. By then, it was looking like a scenario of Whites against Blacks and Asians. The superpower race had inadvertently created a racial world with Whites at the top, Asians in the middle, and the Blacks at the bottom.

Between 1972 and 1975, the Group of Seven (G-7)—the United Kingdom, United States, Germany, France, Italy, Canada, and Japan—was created. The Japanese prime minister was the only one from a non-White country. The inclusion of Japan cannot be dissociated with the economic and military performance of Japan since the 1940s. The Japanese, an Indo-Chinese race, had gained the respect of the Whites during World War II and the fast recovery after their defeat at the hands of the Allies.

The Marshall Plan—in which the United States and the Allied countries invested $600 billion in the Japanese economy—was instrumental and is still considered one of the largest bailouts in history. However, the Japanese people were determined to rebound and worked assiduously at this. They soon began to think they were better than the other Indo-Chinese countries. Sometimes, they even referred to China as the "sick man of Asia." I was in Tokyo in the late 1980s, and the young Chinese, Filipinos, and Koreans all worked menial jobs and could not rise to any higher level because they were "sick."

As a result of the sustained performance in the economy in the 1980s until the 2000s, Japan became the second largest economy in the world, and it was poised to top the world's list if the bubble had not burst in the 2000s. This trend, the performance of China, and the threat of Russian aggression forced Europe, a predominantly White community, to establish the European Union with a unified bargaining power. Race definitions were redefined, and an Indo-Chinese nation was allowed to join the ranks of the White powers in the G-7 because of wealth, knowledge, and negotiation skills. The all-White G-6 accepted a hitherto "lesser race" as an equal. The thaw in ideology had started.

In 1998, the G-7 considered the incorporation of Russia to create the G-8 or G-7 + 1 (Russia). Though Russia is White—and was a superpower at the time—state policy did not encourage open racism. This further strengthened the correlation between Whiteness and superpower status. That China and Japan cannot continue to accept White domineering is seen in the impressive performance of the Asian economies and the challenges in technological breakthroughs and medicine. Together, they made up about 30 percent of the global economy in 2014, and according to the World Economic Forum, it will reach 45 percent by 2050.

In the next twenty years, the African economy will equal the economy of the middle-income countries of Europe today. In fact, according to an estimate by PricewaterhouseCooper in 2008, "The Long View: How Will the Global Economic Order Change by 2050?," and other estimates by the World Economic Forum and *The Economist*, the Chinese economy will become the largest in the world, and it is expected to reach $58 trillion or 20 percent of the world economy. India will be closely second or third. This study still puts the United States at the top of the table by per capita GDP due to the high populations of China and India, making individual Americans still on average some of the richest in the world.

Bravo to the United States for maintaining consistency of the high quality of human life and average productivity for a mixed population. While the average looks good in the United States, other White economies will not be doing as well relative to their competitors. The question then that begs an answer from the White man is how much longer can you claim supremacy? And against whom? African Americans are becoming more conscious of the world's economic and geopolitical arena and will not allow these challenges to go on along the same lines any longer, and the world stage is looking more and more like a battleground of race giants. There are calls for an awakening of the sleeping African giant—just as there were calls for the sleeping China giant to wake up in the 1950s. The White man needs a new strategy in the mixed-race economies of Brazil, the United States, South Africa, the UK, and

France (The *Brusuf* countries) if the overall aggregate production is to be improved and continue to be at the top of nations. We will talk about this in the ensuing chapters.

The so-called sick man of Asia could no longer accept seeing Japan enjoying top seats on the world stage while they with more people had no such status. The battle lines were drawn, and China had to prove that it was awake. The policies of the Communist Party changed several times to adopt more open-door economics while maintaining national unity as a key to sustaining the developmental strides. No dissensions could be allowed to dissuade the course of a ship set to take over the coveted status of number one economy in the world. Being the leading economic powers makes China, Russia, and the United States the three economic superpowers. But is economics the only criteria for being a global superpower?

⊗ What Makes a Superpower?

We will take a few moments to look briefly at what it means to be a superpower. A superpower is a nation with the influence that one state can have over others through its dominance of world trade and economy, world security, world industrial production, development of scientific knowledge, and the propensity to influence other nations to accept the ways of life practiced by the superpower through cultural influence. Superpower status is tied to the hegemony of nations because of political and economic power and dominance.

From the above definition, we can see how the UK, the USSR, and the United States have all gained superpower status at one point or the other—and why Japan, China, and India find it extremely difficult to be true superpowers. Economics alone cannot do it for a nation.

The component dealing with cultural influence and world security is crucial. Rome, Britain, the United States, and Russia all used some element of assimilation and the leverage of language and culture to get global acceptance, but the Indo-Chinese have not traveled along this path. The deep and old culture of these Asian economic giants have stayed intact, and even on overseas missions, a Chinese person would find it difficult to give up his culinary habits to share the tastes of others for a prolonged period. Similarly, Japanese and Indian businessmen and soldiers cannot bring themselves to live among the indigenes of a remote mountainous population and expect to have new families through intermarriages. A few may have done so, but the majority cannot bring themselves to do so.

What are the implications when the Chinese, Indians or Japanese bring their billions of dollars to developing African countries and South America but refuse to share an African meal with the locals for anything more than a week? This shows the lack of the qualities of a global citizen or a global policeman.

In terms of marriages, have you witnessed many Chinese-Black marriages without major backlash back home for both parties? A Chinese friend told me categorically that she might never again be accepted by any Chinese for having dated an African. She had become a pariah. In the larger cities of Tokyo, Beijing, Calcutta, and Mumbai, this is changing, but it's still a long way off before that acceptance that is so critical to world harmony for a superpower can be reached.

The Japanese and German cases are complicated by World War II agreements with the powers then. Due to these two countries working together but losing the war against the Allied powers—the United States, Great Britain, France, and Russia—limitations on their manifestation of military might were imposed. For example, Germany can be an economic superpower—but not a military superpower. Japan has this same limitation, but China and India cannot be limited in this regard. The armed forces of India have participated in UN missions around the world but only in limited coordinated roles. A superpower has to have an independent show of military might to defend certain human rights issues without trampling on the universal rights of others.

In 2017, an African student was dating a Chinese girl. He didn't know she had fallen out with her Chinese boyfriend. The affair went on for close to a year before all hell broke loose. Many women do not have interest in racial issues. As mothers, they see all as one and would soon change to accept anyone who shows care and love. They know that we are all humans and share the same traits of love, intelligence, mercy, kindness, and fear. The issue of skin color does not matter much in a woman's decision when it comes to love. Apparently, this Black-Chinese couple had reached this stage, and the young Chinese man could no longer see them getting back together. He organized with his friends, and they ended up beating the young university student mercilessly. I heard he may have lost his life after that.

The coronavirus pandemic of 2019–2021 was first declared in Wuhan, China, which led to a government lockdown of the city. For two months, no one, including other Chinese people, were allowed into the city. Foreigners left for other cities, and some returned home.

The Africans, on the other hand, stayed, hoping that the health systems in China could handle this outbreak. In 2015, there had been a similar outbreak of severe acute respiratory syndrome (SARS) in China, and the government had succeeded in quelling its spread. So, it seemed this coronavirus, later called COVID-19, was to have been no exception. However, to the surprise and anger of non-racists, at the end of the first wave of the disease, most Africans in Guangzhou, Southern China, were asked to leave their houses and were forced to move to designated areas based only on their countries of origin. Even though some of these persons had stayed in those rented houses for years, their behavior and performance as tenants never impacted the innate impression that the Chinese in that area had of their tenants. Racism got the best of them, and fifty years of efforts by the central government to change the mentality of their people had not succeeded.

The Communist Central Government of the People's Republic of China established a one-country, two-system government in the early 80s and proclaimed a perpetual friend of the African people because of support in joining the UN against the Republic of China on Taiwan. But at the same time, the population however continues to see themselves as Chinese first and global citizens after.

The Chinese government in Beijing sometimes claims that it is not pursuing hegemony, but the result of its impressive economic performance in the past five decades can only result in perceived hegemony. The entire world now accepts China as an economic superpower, but racism continues to permeate its cultural influence over Africa, South America, and Tibet. Of course, while negative racism against Whites is still controlled, as long as the Chinese do not modernize their culture, Indo-Chinese cultural influence on Whites is still a long way off from taking effect. Whites or Blacks will not accept Chinese culture and inculcate them as long as every indication of the lifestyles of the Chinese show a tendency to not accommodate other cultures and races.

Designs of new gadgets are still made in Europe and the United States, but they are fabricated in China—and not vice versa. Europeans and Africans do not wear Chinese clothes. They may eat Chinese noodles and Peking duck in Chinese restaurants, but Peking duck is not on menus in normal European or African restaurants. The problem is that the formula for preparing the dumplings or the fiber for Chinese cheongsam clothing continue to be a mystery that cannot be shared. Europe, Africa, and the rest of the world have opened their doors and shared technology, but the Asians have not.

The United States will send out Peace Corps and the British will send out the VSO, but the Indo-Chinese still need to accept sacrifice for other races outside of their territories without direct economic benefit. At the moment, these countries will continue to listen to the United States and the UK, but they will not take any initiatives on their own with global leadership. This will change in the next twenty years, and by 2040, these countries will be undertaking more global policing and protection of world environments and health security issues as the United States, Britain, and France pull back for lack of the requisite clout and funding.

Based on the above analysis and experience, China, Japan, and India can never achieve true superpower status of the UK, the United States, or Russia! There are no new ideologies to be exported to other nations other than economic expansion and market capture. The proliferation of electronic gadgets from ASEAN countries is merely driven by economics and not humanitarian concern for the world. There is a lack of promotion of world standards in ethics, the environment, and culture.

Typical businessmen from these emerging countries do not apply environmental standards in their development work or respect the preservation of the culture of the locals and indigenes. The primary interest with overseas development work has been economic and political gain. International labor laws and humanitarian feelings toward workers are overlooked, and working conditions are not maintained.

In environmental protection and safety, no higher standards are introduced if this mean financial losses or delays for Chinese businesses. Except on state-sponsored projects, standards are always kept low to cut costs and make more profits. The governments lead the people, but the people do not necessarily follow.

The pie chart in figure 5 shows the distribution of the world's economy in 2019 in PPP terms, and figure 6 shows what is projected for the world in 2050. While the United States has always led the world's economies, this will change from 2022 onward. The People's Republic of China will be the leading economy going forward. The impact of covid-19 on the economies of the white countries has been significant and these countries may not recover their economic status easily.

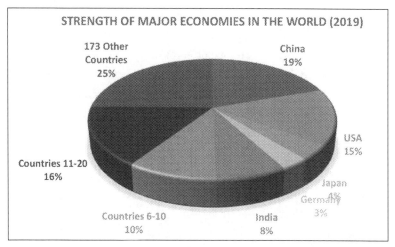

Figure 5: Economy of the large nations in 2019
Source : IMF Statistics, Image by Author

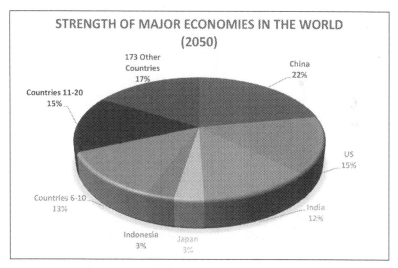

Figure 6: Economy of the major economies, projected 2050

Even though all major industrialized countries will also see an increase in outputs, the Chinese increase will be phenomenal, *ceteris paribus* (all other things remaining equal). This is directly attributable to the per capita output of the citizens.

While the United States capacitates mostly Whites and neglects its minorities, China and India are busy making use of their full complement of human capital and educating their engineers and scientists at the best American and European universities.

The "pull-him-down" syndrome attached to multiparty politics in democracies does not limit the communists as much. China now produces engineers at a ratio of 8:1 compared to the United States and 12:1 compared to Europe. With this army of highly trained professionals all working toward one objective—developing the motherland—it is no surprise that China and India will lead the world in infrastructure and economics.

CHAPTER SIX

Is There a Superrace?

IN TIMES LONG GONE BY, THE TERM *NATION* REFERRED TO A SMALL group of people with similar characteristics and a common heritage and culture. They could have a prominent member with whose name the nation was identified. It was along these same lines that clans were developed. An example of this includes Israel, which was named after the old patriarch Jacob who later became Israel. The Israelites were an assembly of one family, but they were called a nation.

This nation-people nexus has been with us since time began. When nations became larger, and landmarks and historical events determined the names of the settlements, towns, cities, and people became linked to the larger settlement and not to an individual.

Our world is divided into more than 160 nations, each with its own traditions, government, and ways of life. Yet in many ways people throughout the world are very similar. They celebrate joyous events such as weddings and festivals. Actors and singers entertain audiences. Sports enthusiasts cheer their favorite team on to victory. Many of these pastimes have their roots in the distant past. The Olympics for example, began in ancient Greece, while the Inca Sun Festival predates the arrival of Europeans in the Americas. No matter what their origins or nationality, people value their traditions—traditions that have their roots in the thousands of years of history.

—Anatole Mazour and John M. Peoples, *World History: People and Nations* (1993)

Box 2: The world is a mix of races with similarities in lifestyles.

There has always been a strong connection between a nation and its people. As the nations got larger, they broke up and took on newer names, but they had the same families and peoples. The collection was the race. A race of people involves a collection of humans with similar physical features and culture scattered over one continuum of a geographical region or scattered over several discontinuous regions.

In this light, the Indo-Chinese have inhabited China, India, Japan, and the United States, which is thousands of miles away, due to migration. The Caucasians have their kind in Northern Europe, South Africa, and Australia. The members of a race are no longer residing in one small geographical area, constrained by a lack of access to lands, economic opportunities, or legal issues, which is the case for Australia and New Zealand's Caucasians.

The world has become a big global village. Many of the large and most attractive nations for immigrants have ended up with mixed populations and less racism and discrimination, initially changing to a very polarized and racist or discriminatory segregation of people. The nations are no longer reflective of a homogenous people; they have a heterogenous mix of races.

Looking back at the great nations in history, there was always a convergence of culture within the territory. The call for nationalism or the adoption of the vision of a leader was much simpler to achieve. Examples are The Ashantis in Ghana, the Ottoman Empire in Europe etc. Also, this can be seen even recently in Churchill's Britain, Karl Marx's Europe, and Chairman Mao's People's Republic of China. The nation and the races that inhabited them were interlinked and homogenous.

By the eighteenth century—with the discovery of the Americas—things began to change. There was a massive emigration to the New World, especially from Europe. New nations were built where older civilizations existed for hundreds of years in North and South America.

According to John Peoples, author of *World History: People and Nations*, the Inca culture was slowly forgotten and replaced by a mixed European and Inca culture. Old ideologies were dumped, and new approaches to social coexistence were tried out, mixing European, African, and Asian cultures to create new civilizations and economies.

In South America, Brazil is very prominent. It is now one of the most cosmopolitan nations and has complex intermarriages and offspring. The African culture of sport, strong rhythmic music, and dance was introduced to this part of the world, and the culture was forever redefined. The same can be said of Australia, the United States, and even Britain and Europe in general. Mixed cultures have changed the ways of life of the initial inhabitants.

In Europe, in the early part of the nineteenth century, a new interest in Asian culture developed after the adventures of Portuguese and Spanish sailors like Marco Polo. Academics and historians became interested in the concept of an Aryan superrace from India. This race was supposedly migratory and was supposed to have lived in the regions of Iran and India and as far as Central Europe, creating the Indo-European link.

The Germans, Italians, and Austrians discovered the similarities between Latin, Germanic, Greek, and Indian Sanskrit languages. They were so convinced of the existence of such a race of people that the ideology became a national philosophy. Adolph Hitler, Mussolini, and others were enticed into this falsehood of a superrace.

Extended further, this idea goes back to biblical times with the three sons of Noah. The White-skinned brother was considered superior, and the Aryan philosophy preached a preservation of this purity and superiority. Is there really a superrace of Aryans—or is this just Indian mythology adopted and perfected by Caucasians?

In *The Theory of Aryan Race and India: History and Politics,* Romila Thapar opines that further research in craniology showed that European Aryans were different from Asian Aryans. There is no mistaking the fact that the drive to be a colonial power over India led to a strategy of divide and rule, a naked desire to outperform the Indo-Chinese, and a continuous need for recruiting new believers and perpetrators of the ideologies.

If such a superrace existed, why were Indians eventually subdued by the Europeans? Why were they not treated as one of the same kin as their European "Aryan cousins"? Why was civilization in Egypt so much more advanced than in the Indian subcontinent at some time? Why is there a subtle emergence of supremacism in Indo-China today? Is history being repeated with mythology as a new driver of development? India, China, Japan, and the *four tigers*—South Korea, Taiwan, Singapore, and Hong Kong—combined control half of the world's economy. I see the Indo-Chinese leading the world economy but not as a result of the belief in an Aryan superrace.

The above analysis brings us to the situation of the modern world. Over the centuries, various groups of people have come to dominate world politics and the global economy, fueled by racial supremacy thoughts. These periods lasted for hundreds of years, but they eventually waned. New nations evolved with superior technologies and became the dominant power until another power emerges.

The oldest records available to humanity are Sanskrit writings, which are supposedly five thousand years old, and the Old Testament in the Bible, which is seven thousand years old. Which should we accept as factual and reliable? This is a question for individual readers to look into. This book only looks at the facts in front of us, which prove that the races have always been equal and that individuals, groups, and clans have over the years created the impression that one race may be superior to the others in terms of intellect, technological advantages, and military might. The truth is that the top nations have always been those with open policies incorporating the ideas of their citizens in decision-making (inclusiveness) and practicing fair play, the so-called true democracy.

CHAPTER SEVEN

Improving Race Relations for a Better Future of the World

THIS CHAPTER SPEAKS MORE TOWARD THE MULTIRACIAL NATIONS in the world in which three or four races have in large numbers adopted there as a permanent home. These include five key countries: the United States, Brazil, the United Kingdom, France, and South Africa. Of these five, I have only visited the United Kingdom and United States, but I have had working relations with people from these other countries and have seen their approaches to life and the issue of racism.

In all five countries, racism and discrimination exist and are practiced widely. Also, Blacks and other races have lived here for hundreds of years in very deplorable conditions, but through the efforts of international humanitarian organizations, things have changed. Life is getting better, but fear is growing that the "invited guests" are getting more affluent than the hosts. The generations that brought the Blacks and Asians to Europe, South America, and the New World have long passed away, and the White generations of today have no idea how to handle this inequality correctly.

The United Nations confirms discrimination as impacting racism, gender differences, disabilities, and much more. A comprehensive definition is given below: the intended or accomplished differential treatment of persons or social groups for reasons of certain generalized traits. An ever-growing number of terms have been coined to label forms of discrimination, such as racism, sexism, anti-Semitism, homophobia, transphobia, or cissexism (discrimination against transgender persons), classism (discrimination based on social class), lookism (discrimination based on physical appearance), and ableism (discrimination based on disability). (Definition by Brittanica.com).

The Universal Declaration of Human Rights calls on all heads of state and presidents like Donald Trump of the USA and Xi Jingping of China to comply with the United Nations vision of a world without discrimination.

The Universal Declaration of Human Rights calls on all including heads of states and presidents like Donald Trump of the USA and Xi Jingping of China to comply with the United Nations vision of a world without discrimination. The Chinese have been a real disappointment in this regard. After more than seventy years of support from Africans in one of the most difficult periods of Chinese history, since the Communist takeover of China in 1949—the moment they begin to see the light of riches, they returned to the old ways of discrimination and suppression of the very people who fought for their world recognition—and who also are one of their biggest trading partners. China exports $200 billion to Black Africa annually, but it buys only $50 billion from them, causing a trade balance of $150 billion annually. With this amount of net outflow to China, the Chinese people have all the reasons to respect the sweat of the Africans.

Bread and butter are on the table of many Chinese due to the African economy that is still focused on imports, and natural resource prices continue to be undermined by a cartel of Chinese and White people from London, Paris, Berlin, Lisbon and Beijing. The Chinese learned selfish and outright capitalist profiteering from the Europeans, and they are now perfecting the process.

While studying in China, I heard a joke from my Liberian friend that I was never able to confirm. The joke is that in the 1970s, the emerging Communist Chinese government bought one Boeing 737 from the United States. They decided to dismantle the plane and build a Chinese version of it. They painfully copied every detail and manufactured them. They then attempted to reassemble them through experts trained in the best Ivy League universities of the United States.

However, when assembled, the two planes never took off! This was a double loss. All efforts to fly them failed. Frustrated, the leaders eventually agreed to drop their pride and called in Boeing for help. Being the good guys then and wanting to have a bigger market share, Boeing felt obliged to reassemble the planes for a fee. This was a lesson in industrial espionage for the Chinese and for Boeing.

Since then, Boeing always has secret parts that are manufactured and assembled only by top-secret engineers so that they jump out of sync as soon as you try to dismantle them. In Africa, our technicians often say, "The White devil in the gadget returned home." We see that the use of technology has been making the rounds throughtout history. No one race can claim to have it all. The most recent epicenter of technology is in the pacific after having moved from Africa to Europe to the Americas and is now slowly moving to Asia. Did this have to do with races and skin colour? I doubt it. Instead I see a world in which the location of the best engineers and businessmen keeps changing with the times; the most daring and liquid in cash stay at the vanguard of development.

CHAPTER EIGHT

COVID-19 Stokes the Flames of Racism That Still Kindles in the Hearts of Whites

I N DECEMBER 2019, THE WORLD EXPERIENCED ITS FIRST PANDEMIC of the century. From a laboratory in Wuhan, the People's Republic of China, it was announced that a new coronavirus disease (COVID) had been accidentally released. This virus is normally found in animals, but it can be transmitted to humans. The new coronavirus was later dubbed COVID-19, reflecting the year in which it was first detected among humans (2019). This new strain was very contagious and more lethal than the severe acute respiratory syndrome (SARS) and the swine Flu of 2018.

The virus has the potential to suffocate victims and the victim can die within fourteen days. The international medical community knew the significance of this declaration. After two months of observation and projections about the trend of infections, the WHO advised governments all over the world to immediately close down international borders and limit the movement of people within borders as a means of limiting the transmission of the virus.

While swine flu and SARS had only killed six thousand people in one year, COVID-19 infected tens of millions and had killed three million people within six months of its discovery. More details of the virus can be found on the United States Centers for Disease Control (CDC) website: www.cdc.gov.

When it first started as an epidemic, the World Health Organization (WHO) and China's CDC were the leading organizations handling information on the virus until it was reported in other countries in January 2020. Spreading quickly, it was reported in Italy, France, and then the United States. The French still argue that the virus could have been in France two months earlier, in December, but it was was undetected. This is a strange claim. The European medical system and disease tracking are some of the best in the world, but the French were not able to detect it until later. In the end, the world recognized the US claim as the most authentic. The virus originated from a laboratory in Wuhan, China.

In January 2020, no cases were reported in Africa. The virus seemed to be an Indo-Chinese and a Caucasian problem. The health systems in China were overwhelmed, and so were the cases in Europe. The entire Wuhan province, the European Union (EU), and United States declared lockdowns of their countries and airports. Everyone was to stay indoors for weeks and months at a time and not venture outside except for essentials. It was unprecedented in history that so many countries would be in lockdown mode. The airports were silent, and the streets were like graveyards. Traveling risked spreading the virus. Chinese and Europeans were turned away from African airports.

And then things changed. The Chinese claimed that the Africans could be the source of the spread of the virus since only four years earlier there had been the outbreak of Ebola virus in West

Africa. The blame game—or the denial game—had begun. China blamed the United States and other Western countries of spreading the disease, and they also blamed Africa.

The American president did not display diplomacy in March 2020 when he countered and declared publicly at a press conference at the White House that for him the virus was "made in China."

From the superpower attacks and counterattacks, it could be seen clearly that biological warfare was underway. Whoever fired the first shot was going to be investigated and identified. Collateral damage would have to be paid to the entire world if the justice system of the world ever handled such cases. This would be the first of its kind. It would be colossal, considering the number of dead and the impact on the world's economies and the lockdown for three months. Neither China nor the United States would want to pay such huge reparations anyway. In any case, the two suspect countries should lead the process of recovery and pump huge direct capital investments to poorer and hard hit countries to stimulate economic recovery.

The Asians have learned a lot from Europe, and it was high time the Whites learned from the Asians by practicing national racial tolerance as a way of reducing internal tensions. For example, in March and April 2020, Europe and United States condemned the demonstrations of the Chinese in Hong Kong. The People's Republic of China had attempted, in the middle of the worldwide COVID-19 pandemic, to use the opportunity to pass new laws on security that curtailed some freedom of Hong Kong residents. Henceforth, the Mainland Communist Chinese government could have full control of security matters in Hong Kong.

Just one month later, in the United States and the UK, when minorities took to the streets to demonstrate the death of one of their kind, George Floyd—only one week into the Blacks Lives Matter demonstrations—the American Administration in Washington immediately threatened to use the National Reserve and army against demonstrating persons.

The Chinese government and senior officials and Black leaders around the world, in various ways, echoed that the United States should no longer see itself as purely White and the moral guarantor of democracy and human rights if all these incidents of racial killings, deprivation of rights, and suppression of freedom of speech of minorities were happening in its own backyard. Europe and the United States should stop this international diplomacy of double standards of condemning atrocities in Hong Kong but allowing the same neglect of the rights of Blacks, Asians and minority people in Europe and the United States. How much longer can the White man pretend to be superior when all indicators are that we are all equally made with the same cognitive intelligence and emotional intelligence—and we react socially and adversely in the same way when faced with challenges? COVID-19 exposed the racism that still lingers in the hearts of White leaders.

COVID-19 also brought new ways of living. If people traveled between countries, the medical experts required self-isolation for fourteen days.

If you are in public places:

1. Take your temperature with a thermometer as many times as you enter. Report temperatures above 37.5 degrees.
2. Monitor your coughing and report if you have trouble breathing.
3. Stay home and avoid contact with others if you are sick, especially fevers and coughing.
4. Do not use public transportation, taxis, or ride-share services if you can avoid it.
5. Keep a social distance from others of one to two meters at all times.
6. Use a face and nose mask at all times in public.
7. Avoid sending children to schools and colleges.

By late February, the impact on health systems was enormous. In China and the United States, the available incubators and ventilators were not enough to cater for all the sick.

Suddenly, it was a case of prioritizing the treatment and access to ventilators and hospital beds. One of the symptoms of the virus was to inhibit free respiration. Initially, it was widely believed that ventilators helped COVID-19 patients improve their breathing and their chances of survival. In the United States, Brazil, India, and the UK, White nurses gave priority to White patients—to the detriment of Black patients. Racism had been rekindled. More Blacks died of the virus per capita than Whites and Indo-Chinese in mixed-race countries. The racism did not stop with the treatment of Blacks in hospitals. In the streets of the United States and China, Blacks were targeted for attacks.

In the United States, according to CDC reports, the overall cumulative COVID-19 associated hospitalization rate for 2020 was 113.6 per 100,000. People sixty-five years and older had the highest rates with 321.8 per 100,000 followed by people 50–64 years with 171.8 per 100,000. Hospitalization rates are cumulative and will increase as the pandemic continues.

The statistics on COVID-19 infections worldwide as of February 2021 are shown below.

Based on the trends, the cases started in January 2020 very slowly but developed exponentially after April. There will be 120 million infections before the end of 2021, and the number of deaths will hover around 2 percent, meaning a total of more than two and half million dead cannot be far off before the virus can be brought under control and at the end of the virus being any longer a threat, we will see figures of four millions dead. This will not take into account the unreported dead in China, Russia and Africa. This is the worst virus attack in modern history.

In China, in March 2020, African students and tourists in Guangzhou were accused of being suspected carriers of COVID-19 just because they were Black. For years, these students had lived peaceably among the Chinese and their presence was never unwanted—but that didn't matter when faced with the looming threat of COVID-19 and survival of the races. The Africans who had not visited Wuhan were accused of having links to the virus. How could that have happened? The Chinese had been hiding their racial feelings for a long time, but underneath, they never trusted their Black friends. COVID-19 exposed all of this.

As long as international exchanges are ongoing, there's always going to be a need for people from different background, races, and creeds to meet and interact. It's time for people to be judged based on their individual traits and not as a collective of stereotypes.

In faraway countries, this can be exemplified by the events on May 25, 2020. George Floyd, a young Black man, was fatally manhandled by a White policeman in the presence of four other officers in Minneapolis, Minnesota. George Floyd had been suspected of trying to use a fake twenty-dollar bill at a store when the shop attendant called the police. The police had no reason to kill a man for such a minor offense. The overreaction and manhandling were common for White officers handling Black suspects.

While one officer, Derek Chauvin, knelt on the neck of the young Black man for nine minutes, the others, Tou Thao (a Chinese American), J. Alexander Keung (a Chinese American) and Thomas Lane (a White American) did not know what to do and watched by hopelessly confused as to whether to uphold the law for which they were paid and stop their colleague or just let him do what he was doing. In the end, they let him continue, and he eventually killed George to the outrage of Whites and Blacks all over the world. There were mass demonstrations in cities across the United States, London, Paris, Netherlands, Australia, and Africa. These demonstrations were part of the Black Lives Matter movement. Because of George Floyd's death, the world became aware that racism and discrimination were still alive in the world's supposedly most democratic and developed countries, the United States, India, and the UK.

Strangely, in even the eyes of a lion or a tiger, the life of a cub is worth the life of the mother or the father. No human would mess around with a baby lion and get away with it if the father or mother lion were around. In Minneapolis, four officers of the law viewed the life of a human as worth less than twenty dollars.

Racism has made the minds of some Whites so debased that hatred and fear have clouded their reasoning. As I write, the cost of one hour's menial work in the United States is between fifteen and twenty dollars. If the accusation was true, the man could have paid for the damages through forced labor within a day at a quarter wage, but there was no time to work out this mathematics.

This officer was hell-bent on proving that George—with whom he had worked at a previous facility—was no good. As colleagues, he must have eaten from the sweat of George's work for years, but he had forgotten about that. All he saw at that time was Black skin and not the familiar face of George. Was it possible that hatred and jealousy had developed in the days they worked together—and this officer only felt this was his time, now with a badge and a gun, to show him? Why was George trying to pass a fake twenty-dollar bill when he knew there were opportunities all around him? Were there really such opportunities in a country where businesses were closing down? Because of COVID-19, work was stopped. Some people were desperate, but I am not sure George was that desperate.

One month later, another young man was drunk and decided to park his car and take a nap. He parked in a driveway, which caused the fast-food management to call in the police. The police woke him from his sleep and started harassing him. He was forced to drive and was then charged with drunk driving, which the young man rejected. He had been sleeping and not driving drunk. This led to a tussle, and the young Black man wriggled free and ran. The officer could not resist the temptation and shot the young man in the back. The young Black man died later. His crime had been trying to escape from the police accusation of drunk driving.

Even without a degree, anyone can see that the cost of the man's car still parked in the lot was worth much more than the fines that could have been imposed by the courts. Did the police need to use brute force in that situation? No need, I would say. However, because of racism, the officer shot and killed an innocent sleepwalking man.

CHAPTER NINE

A Word for the Wise among the Whites

IN THE MIXED ECONOMIES OF BRAZIL, THE UK, FRANCE, AND THE United States, it must be realized that the race for supremacy is over. The Indo-Chinese have won, and like Usain Bolt heading for the finish line, the Blacks and the Whites have no hope of catching up, except special measures are taken and now.

Based on the forecasts of *The Economist*, the combined economic output of China, Japan, Southeast Asia, and India will reach 60 percent of world total in the next twenty to thirty years. Therefore, the Whites need no longer discriminate against the Blacks and the Hispanics. Instead, they must see that racism against Blacks has only created new economic racial poles: Indo-Chinese and Whites and the whites seem to be on the lower side.

It serves no purpose for the continued hate or fear of Blacks at a time when these White-centric countries need more human resources to boost their output and compete against the fast-growing economies of Southeast Asia. Black people have been residents of these countries for more than three hundred years, and they have contributed to the development of these nations as we know them today.

Many Black heroes have risen the flags of these countries at international events. We can look at the talents of Jesse Owens, Kobe Bryant, Booker T. Washington, Magic Johnson, Usain Bolt, Michael Jackson, Pele, Ronaldo, and Barrack Obama—and the list goes on.

By fairly treating the Blacks without discrimination and creating an environment of peace and mutual coexistence, the human resource bases of the United States, the UK, France, Brazil, India, and South Africa will see a fundamental change within two decades. This will permit slow growth rates to reverse. Production will increase, and living standards will continue to improve.

Whites no longer need to be afraid of their Black neighbors. In South Africa, the Whites who have adopted Africa as their new home will attest that the Africans are a truly friendly people. The same genes in African Americans are in the Blacks on the motherland. They love without question and allow all to live as children of the same father.

I saw other White South Africans trying to avoid the Blacks who attempt to outperform them. Some White man still wants to see the Black man as a slave or a lesser being. This is so shameful in a world that has so much knowledge today, and we all know the truth that four hundred years of slavery permitted this massive difference in economic status. Science has proven that all humans have the same number of teeth and the same amount of blood. Should we continue this exploitation and discrimination? What would the world look like with no racism and no oppression of the rights of racial minorities? Why are ethnic Kurdish minorities in Iraq important, but racial minorities in Africa are not so much? It's because of skin color! Stupid.

The Handbook on Governance Statistics, prepared by the United Nations Human Rights Commission, recommends measurement for the performance of nations along eight dimensions of governance to experience peace and prosperity.

These are the eight pillars on which we can measure nations that have discrimination policies:

- nondiscrimination and equality
- participation in national issues
- openness of institutions to the public
- access to and equality of justice
- responsiveness of governments to their people's concerns
- absence of corruption
- trust in the institutions, such as parliaments, the courts, and the police
- safety and security for all

Properly implemented, the first dimension ensures people of all races, creeds, colors, religions, and handicapped status to be treated equally and fairly and given fair judgment in the justice system. In the United States, one of the biggest problems faced by Blacks and minorities is the fact that once you commit a crime and have been jailed, you have very little chance of getting a good status afterward. The number of minority inmates is so high that if these laws are kept, these young men are forever going to be out of good jobs with the tendency of becoming aggressive and drop outs of society. Rehabilitation in prison should bring about positive change and not more hard-core criminality.

People, and minorities especially, should look forward to life outside prison and contribute meaningfully to society's development instead of being forever frustrated and believing themselves as pariahs in a country where they were born and bred. Why are there better opportunities for those who are not natives? Some see the newly arrived overtaking them quickly, getting better pay, and living in better homes just because they are White.

China uses its minorities to augment its workforce and enrich its culture, getting more income from the tourism, while the United

States and Europe hide a dark chapter of their history. While China has a growing workforce of close to five hundred million persons, the United States and Europe combined can only boast of three hundred million—and the margin is growing. Racism is not helping these economies any longer; it is working against their competitiveness.

Africa and its diaspora communities are a unique collection of minorities. In a world in which the ratio of 8:1 Whites to Blacks exists, the Blacks have unique qualities that have become the envy of the majority, and the majority of Whites do not want to stop until they suppress these people to economic extinction.

UNESCO, which is one of the scientific arms of the United Nations, spends millions of dollars annually protecting snakes species in Brazil from extinction and wetlands in remote locations from pollution and environmental damage, but it does not put in so much effort to secure enough resources to protect the rights of the people in Congo who are threatened with White domination of their bona fide natural resources. The country has become a battlefield of supremacy of the fittest and a haven of oppression as the diamonds and minerals are sought after with impunity.

UNESCO has an obligation to preserve cultures and help improve living standards of minority races around the world and not just the ethnic groups within countries in order to reduce the gaps in the Gini coefficient. While the UN Charter preaches equality of all people as a fundamental right, they use mild diplomatic means to communicate with arrogant ultra-racist leaders to treat the Black continent unfairly in business, world trade, and opportunities. This approach can never yield the right results within our lifetimes. It has taken four hundred years to stop slavery, and if reversing it is going through the same procedures, it could be at least a hundred years before we see equality as we want it.

The African economy has grown in the twenty-first century but not so much from the efforts of the United Nations as from self-awareness and bootstrapping. According to world-renowned economists like Akinwumi Adesina of the African Development

Bank and the experience of development practitioners working on changing Africa, we can see that a complex web of factors will have to be taken into consideration to ensure the transformation of Africans and their self-esteem. This will be addressed in the ensuing chapters.

This brings in the UN's Sustainable Development Goal 11: Reduce income inequalities across nations. The clarion call has been sounded, but who is heeding it among the leading Western and White countries? The IMF conditionalities for loan disbursement are always draconian against African countries. The World Bank limits the amounts of loans a country can be allowed in any one year—while other countries are allowed to print as much money as they find necessary on the grounds that the absorptive capacity of Black economies has been saturated. These double standards are intended to limit the expansion of the continent and must be reversed. Every banker knows that kick-starting a business requires capital infusion and not roadblocks. Why is the World Bank any different? It's high time for a new model of financing investments in developing countries, with particular considerations for Black economies, be developed by the Bretton Woods Institutions.

The World Economic Forum has identified forty-six factors for development of the African continent's economies. It is beautifully captured in the figure below.

These factors have been classed into eight subgroups that focus on economic development. It is true that Africa urgently needs to develop economically along these forty-six factors, but they do not fully address the underlying problems of the continent's poor performance and the situations of Blacks globally.

These are high-level issues, and a top-down approach works only after the bottoms-up approach (see next chapter) has been tried out:

1. A Secure Africa
1.1 International Security
1.2 Geopolitics
1.3 Role of Religion

When it comes to economic issues, the world truly needs a *new political order* with a rights-based and raceless society. To resolve this, the five major mixed-race economies and India should immediately and unequivocally commit to the Blacks and Hispanics and give them the same opportunities and responsibilities expected of the Whites in these countries. Most Whites would claim Christianity as their religion, but they do not have the desire to listen to the Christian God's call for a fair and just world. This is hypocritical.

Martin Luther King Jr. had a dream where he saw Blacks and Whites walking side by side. By investing in education scholarships, equal pay opportunities, sharing information, and equal participation in national issues, these nations will ensure improved performance of their economies as the productive capacity—and GDP will soar proportionately to the increase in labor.

The People's Republic of China has sixty-six ethnic groups, and the Han is the largest. The Han speak Mandarin Chinese. The Muslims and other ethnic groups in the northwest part of the country are considered minorities. In the 1980s, the Communist Party of China realized that the Han ethnic majority alone could not make a strong Chinese nation while the minorities were left behind. The government invested massively in Tibet, Urumqi, and Inner Mongolia and transformed an ancient culture and civilization into a modern one with some elements of the past left for cultural preservation and tourism. The result within four decades was a prosperous Chinese nation that is poised to topple the GDP (in real terms) world table in a few years, say 2030.

Some Chinese, Japanese, and Asians do not seem to have racial preferences in business, but if they see a White race that is tolerant of Blacks, they will also practice similar policies. For now, as long as Europe continues on its mission of clandestinely raping the African continent and their persistent hidden agenda of suppression, the Chinese and Indians will copy suit—and so will the Arabs. Europe will continue to fall economically relative to their Asian counterparts, and the five multiracial countries dominated by Whites will not experience peace and fast growth. They will always wonder why the Asians seem to be flourishing more.

Reflections

For behold, I am for you, And I will multiply people on you ...
The cities shall be inhabited and the waste places rebuilt.
—Ezekiel 36:9–10

Sing like no one's listening, love like you've never been hurt,
dance like nobody's watching, and live like it's heaven on earth.
—Author unknown

CHAPTER TEN

A Word for the Wise to the Black Man in Africa and the Diaspora

THIS CHAPTER PROVIDES INSIGHTS INTO SOME OF THE PRINCIPAL causes of the failures of Blacks in the world and to propose ways to improve performance. There have been many economic analyses of the causes of failure of the African continent. Some were listed by the World Economic Forum in the last chapter but not discussed in detail. Other attempts have been made in the book, "Why Nations Fail".

The root causes of this failure are more humanistic and artificial than is often recognized. Failure itself has been looked at as only poor economic performance and the inability of governments to meet the needs of the citizenry. Deeper root causes have often been overlooked by Western analysts. In this chapter, which is the largest, we have brought out the issues as never before seen.

Western and Asian nations today have mega-multinational companies, some with capital approaching $200 billion or above. More and more such giants are being created by mergers and acquisitions. The negotiating power of such White businesses are so large that there can be no hope for Black economies if the superpower race and consequent economic racism continue to top their agendas.

The African is daily asking, "Oh, God, why are we suffering so much?" The answer is there on the wall. There is a concerted and coordinated effort to outperform one another in the unspoken global racial wars, and the Africans are still sleeping, hoping to be awakened at the end of the race. It's time to awake, Africa, from your slumber! The other armies are marching on.

On its website, the African Development Bank (AfDB) declares that it was created in the 1960s to spur economic development and social progress among its member countries. These incidentally happen to be the least developed countries in Africa—and the least developed in the world. There is a link between the work of the African Development Bank, the European Development bank, the Inter-American Development Bank, the New Development Bank, and other regional banks and racism. At this high macroeconomic level, the multilateral development banks make commitments and invest huge sums of money in some cases to help Africa, but the continent still records lackluster progress compared to its Asian counterparts. The New Development Bank wants to change all of this.

Figure 7: Heads of States (from L to R) of Russia, India, Brazil, China and South Africa (The BRICS) Meeting in 2014- a rare show of unity of the races

For example, the African Development Bank has planned an investment of $1.5 billion to $2.8 billion to fund the transformation of African agriculture in the African Agriculture Transformation program (TAAT). The new governor of the bank initiated a high-five strategy to address his top five priorities for Africa: to light up and power Africa, to feed Africa, to industrialize Africa, to integrate Africa, and to improve the quality of life of the people of Africa. Five simple, strategic, and highly focused objectives and many more initiatives from sons of the continent have benefitted millions in Eswatini, Zambia, Sudan, etc. With the World Bank's involvement in poor, highly indebted, less developed countries (HIPCs) for so many decades, there should have been changes, but this is not still seen in Africa.

There must be other reasons for the poor performance we see in these countries. Is it that Africans do not love development? Are they happy being at the bottom of the Global Development Index ladder and by extension the creators of the economic racism against them? The answer to both questions is no. Africans are a proud people who love development and love nature. They are willing to work to change the status quo, but their hands are tied.

I have always believed that, as Africans and Blacks also, we owe to ourselves the biggest responsibility to develop self-esteem and lift the banner higher. As much as I hate to discriminate against other ethnic groups in my home country, I also think it's bad that the world of Whites discriminates against Blacks because of skin color—and some Blacks try to copy Whites by reciprocating. Should I then become racist also and join the ranks of superficial-minded humans? No. May it not be my portion that I will join the ranks of those who see other humans as inferior when we have seen Bill Clinton rising from nothing to become president or Barack Obama rising from the son of an immigrant in Hawaii to become president.

On the other hand, to see others as incompetent cannot be excluded from a man's thinking. Incompetence is born from lack of personal endeavor and training and a lack of the will to deliver. Along these lines, therefore, as previously expounded in the chapter on superpowers and race relations, Whites are tempted to overlook or even discount Black inputs into the world's development. So many upstart Whites are catered for and given support until they come to maturity and stature. Some may not look at the root causes of these poor performances or just ignore the facts and continue to despise a people because of the color of their skin and their competence levels. They fail to see the repeated attempts to suppress anything made in Africa—even humans—through entry barriers and oligarchies.

As soon as you paste "Made in Africa" sticker on a piece of clothing or shoes, the chances are they will no longer sell. It happened to China in the 80s. The strategy was to stop labelling and just sell until people got convinced of the quality. Then suddenly, the branding came again. Infinity Motor Company used the same tactics to change the mentality of Europe and the Americas against Japanese products. Africa should try its secret marketing strategy to gain market share and then disclose the sources.

A case comes to mind vividly when I worked at the London

Mining Company. In 2013, the company was into the mining of iron ore. The target production was five million tons per annum. The operations and maintenance expenses (O&M) were almost 60 percent of the gross income. Of the two thousand direct workers, there were twenty-one managers of departments, and only two of these were Black Sierra Leoneans, including me. Every day, the pressure was to meet the daily production targets, and anyone who did not perform could be replaced with one day's notice.

All went well at the start with East European directors until the South Africans took over the directorship. Within a month of taking over, they were replacing 30 percent of the managers, both Black and East Europeans. Racism had come to London Mining. There was to be no sympathy in business. Though the company had succeeded for several years under the various directors, it had to be White or nothing. All key positions were replaced with White South Africans until we had to invoke the Local Content Act, which secured 20 percent of senior positions and 80 percent of junior positions for nationals—thanks to our forefathers who had foreseen such future trends.

A lot of Africans and Blacks have made it big in the corporate world. Look at the achievements of modern-day Blacks such as Kofi Annan at the United Nations, Barack Obama, Mohamed ElBarradei, Kandeh Yumkella, Davidson Nicol, Michael Jordan, Oprah Winfrey, Whoopi Goldberg, Mo Ibrahim, Aliko Dangote, all the African presidents, Julius Maada Bio, Ellen Johnson Sirleaf, and the engineers who built the highways and hotels in Africa. There is enough justification to see that Blacks can make it better than millions of Whites.

The issue today is not about whether some individual Blacks can be better than individual Whites in terms of economic performance, technological contributions, inventions, or intellect. The challenge is in the numbers of such people, the average economic performances of Blacks, and future prospects. As long as the majority of Blacks remain poor, the hard work of the other few will not be recognized.

In the past three decades, the four Asian tigers and Singapore, Brazil, South Africa, Nigeria, and Botswana improved their economic performance from developing country status in the 1960s to emerging economies by 2000 with a bias toward developed country status. We can conclude without fear that development to a middle-income or developed-country status is only two or three generations away in a well-coordinated and planned economy. This conclusion also applies to individuals whose fortunes can change in a short space of five to ten years with determination, perseverance, and Godspeed.

The twenty-first-century world is dominated by science, high-speed internet, and financial tools that run the global marketplace and ensure sustainable development of the continent. Africa's growth has to be accelerated to stop being the "sick continent of the world," to borrow from Asian phraseology.

PART TWO

So, What Should Africans Do?

CHAPTER ELEVEN

A New Approach to Transformation for the African Continent

THE SOLUTIONS TO AFRICA'S WOES ARE PLENTY, BUT THERE should be a continuous effort to try out new ways and new outlooks. As a result, I will leave the forty-six-point World Economic Forum (WEF) analysis, previously outlined, for the macroeconomists and try to develop a simpler list that incorporates the twenty key factors that the average African perceives are the problems impeding the continent's performance at a micro level. Some may overlap with the WEF factors, which is fine, but I have tried to analyze these from a racial perspective, which will allow a lens that only a few people can see through—and only some people will say what they really see when they look through the same lens.

These thoughts come in seven categories:

1. Cultural Transformation
2. Appropriate Legal Framework
3. Reevaluation of the Values of the Black Man
4. Economic Improvement
5. Welfare of the Population
6. Improving Competitiveness
7. New Approach to Politics

This can be called the **"CARE to WIN" Approach.**

We will take each and further decompose it to provide a comprehensive analysis.

1.Cultural Transformation

It can be argued that the sociocultural background of Africans was completely altered during the past four hundred years in ways that cannot easily be determined today. It may be impossible—or even unnecessary—to recreate what existed then, but it is important to see a correlation between the Black social culture and the role it plays in development. Certain traits need to be reviewed to meet the modern trends of acceptable social behaviors.

The sociocultural transformation elements under review are:

1. Review of the Extended Family System
2. Wasted Youth Productivity
3. Impact of Overreliance on Tradition

1.1 Review of the Extended Family System

The idea of family in Africa meant each was related to other relatives. While this created opportunities for a network, in times of need, it also had the major disadvantage of taking away a lot of resources from the immediate family. Economists call this reverse situation "the demographic dividend within the family."

With Africans having less and less extended family in the future, it is expected that the dividend will be higher, and there will be more disposable income for the immediate family. This condition has been shown to be impracticable in Africa when people feel obliged to cousins, uncles, aunts, and grandparents.

This perception has to change, and the finances of the family have to be managed in such a way that the well-being of the immediate family is guaranteed while maintaining the culture of the extended family. This is only possible if African governments improve on their social welfare programs, taking care of the elderly, orphans, and widows.

Along this line of thought, people of African descent have to look at a new proposed alternative to nuclear family systems as a way of increasing the availability of capital for development. The new African type of nuclear family should be redefined to include the father, the mother, the children, the grandfathers, and the grandmothers. The lack of amenities for the aged and the respect for the elderly mean African nuclear families do not allow their weak or vulnerable parents to go through the kind of abandonment seen in the West. An idle mind is the devil's workshop and a quick route to extinction. The parents should be kept busy, active and strong to prolong their lives. To make them partially productive therefore, they would have roles like caregiving to grandchildren and being homemakers in their children's homes whenever possible. The children should make provision for regular allowances. Better still, governments should make provisions for elderly people above 60 years' old or vulnerable adults who register for support.

1.2. Wasted Youth Productivity

Blacks waste a lot of time sitting and arguing in tea shops sipping "artire,", watching international football leagues, drinking and merrymaking, taking drugs, telling stories about what happened to their heroes years ago, prancing around in a violent manner, and engaging in other debilitating acts instead of engaging in productive acts and trying to invent or discover new things for income generation and wealth creation.

Studies such as "Labour Productivity and Employment Gaps in Sub-Saharan Africa" by Ellen McCullough of Cornell University and the World Bank have shown that Black youth productivity is less than their Asian counterparts, and the Africans tend to focus on agriculture and storytelling, which are more labor intensive or low in output.

African government statistics and publications are mostly unreliable and at times distorted and do not report the true facts due to political manipulation. This has contributed to the frustration and laid-back attitudes these youth show in Africa. The political class is only interested in their votes rather than helping them become better citizens in their communities. Therefore, these youth soon lose interest in their national development agendas and take to storytelling and day dreaming becoming rich and living the highlife without substance to back these dreams.

Governments in Africa and other mixed-race governments must have specific and targeted programs that will help transform Black youth and can be sustained over the years. The Japanese, under the Marshall Plan, instituted a scheme for their youth, and that created the technological power they are today.

Africa can pay back its debts if investments are not tied to huge donor salary professional inputs. Because of this, funds have not been used in direct benefit items. The Paris Declaration on Aid Effectiveness is clear on these points and must be used in such investments. This is not to say Blacks do not need the expertise of White expats. It is about the disparity in salaries between the locals and expats. The American Peace Corps program, though often accused of including spies, is one of such expertise that Africans look forward to. How about an African pool of expats? From within and from the diaspora, as suggested by Ambassador Dr. Arikana Chihombori-Quoa. Instead of idling in the diaspora after retirement, please come home and join this corps of professionals.

1.3. Impact of Overreliance on Tradition

In African cultures, the young should "tread warily in the presence of elders." People say, "If you know how to wash your hands, you can eat with the elders." These sayings only hold sway in the premillennial era. In the age of the internet and the information superhighway, youth cannot afford to wait for "slow-moving" adults to make decisions for them. They need experience as the best teacher. It will be premature, at this stage, to say the old-fashioned ways had no merits. Therefore, a blend between the culture of respect for traditions and the desire to outperform on the world stage is a must.

The world seems to be moving in one direction. It is driven by an endless quest for wealth and the propensity to consume. Whites are willing to come to Africa to work for Africans if it means a better income. Thousands of consultants are flocking in daily, looking for opportunities that can enable them to pay the mortgage that has eluded them for years and have the chance to finally own their dream houses.

The White consultant does not look at the idea of working for and under Blacks; he looks at his pay master and does what he is paid for. Some come at a young age and work for young Blacks. As soon as the work is done, they put on an air of pride and head for the Whites-only club in a suburban area.

In contrast, African elders often do not take instructions from younger kin. Because of this, there is often friction in the early stages of the boss-and-subordinate relationship akin to the forming and norming stages of Tuckson's team building stages. When this is overcome, the work then goes smoothly, but the performance at work is mostly slow.

The solution has been to have older people be the bosses, but this arrangement will not be tenable for much longer. With Africa's younger generation populating the continent, the UN Population Fund statistics show there is a median age of eighteen to twenty-five. Africa and Asia will have the youngest workforces in the world by 2050 if present population trends continue. Therefore, these traditional barriers to collaboration and work ethics are being challenged. Younger graduates are taking up senior and more challenging positions.

Less experienced in the Internet of Things (IoT), the elders will have to undergo a major cultural paradigm shift and support the younger ones who are tech savvy and prone to better use the new technologies in the accelerated developments seen today.

2. Appropriate Legal Framework

One of my old mentor often reiterated that organizations are strong with the existence of strong laws and the willingness to enforce them on members. This can be extended to the national context and corporate environments.

If success is going to come to African communities, the virtues that once held the large kingdoms and emirates of Sokoto in Nigeria together have to be revisited.

The following legal frameworks come to mind in the quest for the Black man's reassertion:

1. Corporate Protection Laws
2. Corruption Management
3. Competitiveness

2.1. Corporate Protection Laws

The global economy is moved by large, multinational organizations. In 2018, the Hong Kong and Shanghai Banking Corporation (HSBC) and the Bank for International Settlements (BIS) estimated that more than $5 trillion in currency transactions moves across the globe daily. To ensure the success of these transactions, strong corporate laws to protect investments and uphold transactions are needed so that the transactions go as expected. Otherwise, as has been seen, Ponzi schemes will develop—and funds could be diverted elsewhere with impunity.

In preparation for expansion and development, Africans should adopt strong banking and corporate laws to protect direct foreign investments (DFIs) as they move funds into the continent. In the UK and the United States, rich White women clutch their bags when they see a young Black man approaching. I was shocked in London when a White lady clutched her bag and looked at me from the corner of the eye. It felt as if she were saying to herself, "Do you think I will let you take this bag away?"

Looking at her quizzical eyes, my mind replied to her unasked question: "What can I do with the little you have in your bag, White lady? I am a prince, the son of a King, the Most High God. I personally paid for my plane ticket from Africa to London—not to snatch a bag but to find out what I can take back home, that which your forefathers have taken from our great grandfathers. I can do this through technological transfers and long-term business relations. I am not interested in the peanuts found in handbags." This self-declaration pleased me enough to forget about the incident, but these incidents repeat themselves every now and again in different places around the White man's world. By 2012, I was very much involved in looking for investments in the housing business in Ivory Coast. I sent out requests to friends and relatives to help locate investors. After making much headway, one of the potential investors, interested in gold, told me gold from Africa changed many times into dust between the African airport and European airport. He would prefer if we transported the gold to Europe first and were paid there. I tried convincing him—to no avail. My investor friend was confident in the laws of Europe but not in those of Africa, and we could not provide him comfort or have the funds to prefinance the trip. The deal failed and was terminated. Later, I was told to go through the Ghana Precious Mineral Marketing Company (PMMC) to get government-supported transactions. The only problem was that I had lost my investor.

The PMMC has two key functions:

1. Grading, assaying, valuing, and processing precious minerals.
2. Buying and selling precious minerals.

Other countries have similar structures. Sierra Leone has the Government Gold and Diamond Company (GGDO), which investors have used to avoid problems, and others have used registered businesses with fixed addresses.

African and Black governments should ensure protection of all forms of investments and raise confidence levels in order to attract the inflows of investments that are badly needed to create jobs and exports. In other sectors of internet banking and money transfers, similar structures need to be developed and corporate laws for acquisitions and mergers, protecting small businesses and mining operations for Africans must be set up.

2.2 Corruption Management

The points expressed here on gold transactions paint a grim possibility of foul play by state officials against foreign investments. This elevates the need to curb corruption in Africa more than any other concern in Africa. The E.SUN Bank has a very proud statement: "Our operations are conducted with the highest standards of integrity, and our brand is built on exemplary professionalism."

I have seen similar statements across the business spectrum in Africa, but the commitments to stand by such ethical statements remain a huge stumbling block. Hence, the anti-corruption agencies should be put to task because, according to the World Bank estimates, corruption has cost countries 10–15 percent of their GDP and has driven away serious institutional investors.

To me, corruption is a two-way street between the receiver and the giver. It can either be an investor and a government official, an employee and a client, or two employees conniving for individual gain. In the end, society needs people who can conform to principles, persons of integrity, people will be self-satisfied with whatever result of a process or application, and people who accept the results no matter how disappointing or embarrassing they may be.

The challenge in Africa has been that there has not been a culture of integrity since independence in the 1960s. Burkina Faso was known as Upper Volta until Thomas Sankara, the revolutionary leader, changed the name. It is one country out of fifty-eight predominantly Black countries, including those in the Caribbean, which has stuck to the principle of integrity to this day. They refer to their country as the "Country of the People of Integrity." They try to be faithful to their words even in adverse conditions or when faced with poverty.

In Mainland China, government workers—even under draconian Communist measures—have been a people of integrity. The Confucian principles of frugality instilled in them at an early age stay on through adulthood. Of course, times are changing very fast with Western ideological influence.

Africa needs similar development foundation and strong anticorruption laws. Unfortunately, Africans did not all develop under the same system. The Francophones, Anglophones and Lusophones have different legal and economic systems that need harmonization before a total unification. The French for example see a person as "guilty until proven not guilty" while the English see you as "not guilty until proven guilty". These are two sides of the same coin but need to be understood in the various contexts.

3. Reevaluation of the Values of the Black Man

For four hundred years, the Black man has undergone suppression, humiliation, oppression, and exploitation at the hands of fair-skinned humans. This has forced many Blacks to compensate for feelings inferior, but many Blacks have remained timid and subjugated, which makes a reevaluation of the worth of the Black man necessary. This can be done through four actions:

1. Raising Awareness
2. Raising the Value of the Black Race
3. Thinking Big
4. Adopting High Moral Values and Trust

3.1 Raising Awareness

Governments around the world should be bold enough to accept that slavery took place and acknowledge that it affected the lives of the Blacks around the world to the point that some still find themselves stranded in faraway lands, including Jamaica, Guyana, Brazil, England, and the United States. Many continue to live in abject poverty and lack opportunities. If they had stayed in their countries, some would have been among the elders of their countries.

In the decades following the independence of African nations, there was a de facto acceptance that independence meant the end of the vestiges of slavery and colonialism. It turned out to be a big mistake. There was still more work to do. The African Union, through the United Nations, should ensure that nations that benefitted from slavery and colonialism pay. This would help redress the inequalities that have arisen from this ugly historical event.

There should therefore be a truth and reconciliation approach to the economic empowerment of the African continent and the rebranding of the Black race. At the moment, donor aid, though trickling in, seems not to be impacting the development of the countries very much. Where is the African Marshall Plan?

3.2. Raising the Value of the Black Race

Drawing from the awareness and acceptance that the Blacks underwent major losses in their economies and family systems during slavery and colonialism, the world system should move toward redefining the worth of the Black man.

An incident I encountered comes to mind. In 2012, while at the African Minerals Mining Company Limited (AML) in Sierra Leone, I was the only Sierra Leonean Technical manager out of 14 managers responsible for the construction of the 192-kilometer railway line from Pepel to Tonkolili. I was responsible for more than two thousand staff, both expatriate and nationals.

Because I had a Sierra Leone passport when I arrived from volunteering for the United Nations Volunteers in Burundi and Ghana, I was offered a "National Pay Scale" while the expatriates were offered "Expatriate Pay Scale." In fact, I was not allowed to see their salaries to prevent me from complaining. However, since I was the department's manager, I had access to the department's budget from which I could estimate the average expat's salary. I was able to find out that the expatriate engineers I was supervising were receiving about two times my salary, and other managers, my level, who were expatriates received about three times my salary!

I summoned the courage and asked my supervisor, the general manager, and he gave me the dumb reason that these expats had their homes and children in schools in Europe and the United States and had more expenses. I showed him that my children were also in the United States, China, and the Philippines and explained that I wanted to do a long-distance PhD in Europe, but he paid no attention to my revelation and intention. Instead, he countered that national regulations would not allow locals to be paid as much as their expatriate counterparts. All my efforts, therefore, were in vain.

One of the staff at a state-owned enterprise (SOE) in Sierra Leone in 2020, after three years working with a consultant who had spent fifteen years in Africa, stated with frustration:

> The consultants came here, took our knowledge,
> and gave them back to us in the form of documents.
> They knew nothing—but ended up being the
> experts. They get all their ideas from us through
> engagements and interviews but claim superiority.
> We know our local environment better, and our
> leaders can do far better.

While this, in itself, shows prejudice, it reflects, more and more, Black consciousness and an awareness to reclaim its worth and work toward Black nations being more responsible for their growth and self-realization than ever before.

In another incident, a reputable international bank was to open offices in an African country. They proposed a salary scale that they believed was appropriate for the work to be done, but the government officials, for some strange reason, would not authorize the salary scale. The bank also thought there would be too much operational risk involved if low salaries were paid to its workers. Therefore, the bank did not go ahead with the project; it did not operate in the country.

I took it then that the bank had more concern about the welfare of the national staff than the government did. The common belief is that higher salaries encourage a flight of personnel from the government to the private sector because there are better wages. In a free market, the government should not regulate the sector to the point of pegging salaries. The governments should allow independent and private companies to operate without much control. The push-and-pull forces of demand and supply should determine and set the appropriate salary scales on which the sector should operate. As a preventive measure, rules governing movement and rotation of staff can be put in place to maintain sanity.

A contrary incident to the above happened with another foreign company. The governments had set a minimum salary scale. No matter who came for work, the company only added a small fraction to the minimum wages, but the company defended its action as being in line with government regulations, a common line of defense put forward by strict communist countries.

Another incident is the African women who spend billions of dollars on various hairstyles just to look like White, Chinese, and Brazilian women—a thing White women will never reciprocate. According to the Euromonitor International and Reuters news agency, the money spent on artificial beauty in the form of hair, eyelashes, fingernails, and skin-lightening creams is a staggering $6–8 billion industry per year in Africa. This is more than the GDP of small nations of the World. That money could have been used to develop small businesses in the respective African countries and improve educational levels. Unforgivingly, the educated Black women are the first to be brainwashed, making them feel that their short, kinky hair is not beautiful enough and that they need long hair to be classy. This is a betrayal of Black beauty and an awful waste of scarce resources. Some women argue that White women also tan their skin to look darker, but this is not true. The tanning is more for medical reasons than aesthetics alone.

Unfortunately, it's the men who pay for this and allow this trend to continue. Equally so, men do waves and curls on their natural hair, but they maintain and pay for their women's false hairs to look foreign. Only the African men can change this by refusing to pay for the false hair, rejecting them and instead investing in improving the natural hair.

African governments should see the Black man as important and as valuable as any other humans on Earth. A very popular African parable states, "If the house does not sell you, the street cannot buy you." It seems again that these governments have been brainwashed to believe that their people are inferior and have lower performance comparable to White workers and must be paid less. Sadly, this belief and action have been supported by organizations such as the African Development Bank and the United Nations. It is now a matter of redefining Africa, and then all other negative perceptions will change.

Recently, I looked around my office and observed that all the equipment and furniture were imported. I looked at my clothes, my shoes, my socks, and my underwear—all imported! I went into the other directors' offices. It was the same. I then went to the canteen. I felt slight relief as a few items on the table decorations had been made in Africa. The dependence on foreign-made goods is endemic in Africa. In Sierra Leone, it is seen fashionable to go for "not made in Sierra Leone" things. We have refused to buy homemade items. I, henceforth, resorted to having African tailors for my clothing, African cobblers for my shoes, and local carpenters for my household decorations and furniture.

Obviously, the donor funds can only cover 10–15 percent of basic needs in these countries. The African Union's "Free Trade Agreement" has not been enough when the Blacks still harbor the belief that only imported items are best. The imported items are better and more durable, but there is more Africans can crave than quality and durability. There is a need to raise Africa's value, which supersedes the trivial value of self-gratification.

African governments are gradually passing indigenous products regulations that are enforceable and moving toward gaining parity of status for locals with expatriates in the workplace, whereby salary variances should not exceed 20 percent of the local workers' salaries for expatriates.

African governments should pass laws mandating a minimum of 30 percent of public purchases to be internally produced goods to reduce consumption of foreign exchange and improve African enterprises. At the same time, standards must be enforced to ensure value for money.

Already existing local content laws should be enforced to help Africans catch up. The African Union should introduce the monitoring of national spending on local products. Except for high-tech products like computers, cars, and planes, basic commodities, food, and goods production should be made or done in Africa. In addition, value added in Africa should be ensured from 2021 until 2063. In essence, we instill in the minds of public officials and patriotic Africans a pride for "made in Africa." When we go back to the first principle of development, self-reliance, and redesign Africa's growth path, we can afford to buy European or American products. For now, we are only able to buy Chinese products.

3.3. Thinking Big

Born in an African home, I have seen how long it took for Africa to reach where it is today. That painstaking slowness was caused by governments that engaged in thinking small instead of big and thinking slowly and introspectively instead of fast and retrospectively.

The World Bank and the African Development Bank, in the 2015 African Competitiveness Report, concluded that productivity in Africa had stalled in the past decade—and that productivity of Asian labor was overtaking Africa's. Part of the reason it put forward was that Africans continued to think small and were not improving their productivity fast enough.

In *Think Big*, Dr. Benjamin Carson challenges us all to think bigger than normal and that any well-thought-out plan can become a reality. For him, the only limit is one's imagination. As someone once said, "If you can imagine it, then you can make it happen."

The ten steps for realizing big dreams are as follows:

1. 1. Think out all the needs and options and choose a big plan.

2. Write out the plan and the goals to be achieved with time frames.

3. Set out the activities that will enable you to achieve your plan in the best order to be implemented. Each big achievement is called a milestone.

4. Commit the resources you have and start something—no matter how small. If you have to build a house, start by buying the land, making a blueprint, or drawing the plan.

5. Write them down, print them out, and hang them on a wall or put them in your diary—and then look at them regularly.

6. Follow up on the activities daily, weekly, or monthly to ensure you are making progress toward your goal.

7. Pray over your plans daily and ask the Lord to help you overcome the obstacles and open doors for your success. Prayer works miracles and opens doors you never thought of.

8. Check regularly if you are achieving the milestones in the time frames. If not, adjust the times and commit to meeting the next time frame.

9. Celebrate each time you reach a milestone. Be pleased with yourself.

10. Once complete with the first big thing, set in motion the next big plan—and then return to step 1.

Think big, dream big, believe big—and the results will be big. African cities can be big. Salaries can be sustained at high levels if the Blacks put their minds to it. You can always have big plans throughout your life. Only with those big plans will the world be a bigger place for all.

Closely related to this is Africa's role in geopolitics. For too long, the African Union has worked on unity on the continent. As a result, it has shied away from their other roles globally.

As home to 20 percent of the world's population and natural resources, there is need for the AU to give more consideration to its strategic role in world politics. In the Security Council of the United

Nations, the five permanent seats include three White nations (UK, France, and Russia), one Asian (People's Republic of China), and one mixed (United States).

The technological and economic performance of the continent seems to be militating against Africa's strategic influence. To fully assume its role, Africa's leading nations like Nigeria, South Africa, and Egypt will have to stand out and participate more in global security and engage in humanitarian relief operations, similar to what the five superpowers always do: showing concern over natural disasters, boosting the economies of failing nations, contributing to world peace, and the like.

African leaders should stop looking only within their limited confines. They need to think big, bold, and beyond the borders of the continent. The world is for all, and successful Black nations should stand to help other continents and peoples in need. Blacks should start playing the game of geopolitics and make sacrifices that are worthy of the status of world leaders. Only when they begin to do so will other races accept the Black race as equals. This should not be just through mere logic of proportional representation as is now being argued in some circles. The AU should be seen as going beyond the competence of logic and physically help quell wars wherever they break out in the world. Let the laboratories of Africa work to develop a world-class cure for COVID-19. Let there be a space program funded by Africa. That is expected of a people who aspire for recognition.

Alas, in Africa, we seem to be forever solving bread-and-butter issues as the Western and Asian countries are manufacturing millions of cars and ships. Though they have limited minerals, Western nations still have the world's largest factories. African nations have plenty of minerals, yet they do little with them.

Africa has all 102 elements of the periodic table in commercial amounts, yet we do nothing but sell them out. We have the best fish in the world, but we sell them out and grapple with malnutrition. We have the most pristine environments in Africa, Brazil, and the

Caribbean, yet we endure the wanton destruction of our forests and ecosystems. There is, indeed, need for reawakening if Africa wants to compete in the global arena.

Awake, O, Africa. Forget the past abuses and suppressions and start afresh. The sky is the limit.

3.4 Adopting High Moral Values and Trust

Due to marginalization, poor performance, and discouragement, lifestyles change—and the weaker ones lose moral ground. Blacks have been known, in mixed racial countries, to resort to violence, guns, and drugs to escape the rigors of life. Indeed, Blacks have been unfairly and mercilessly mistreated, thrown out in the cold, jailed, and murdered in White countries for them trying to cross borders.

Blacks will continue to stay in countries where they were former slaves, but governments in mixed racial countries—the United States, India, Brazil, South Africa, the UK, France, Jamaica, and other Caribbean nations—should create a conducive environment that will rehabilitate, rather than torture, them. Doing so creates a new culture with high moral values that trusts its government because it considers minorities integral and useful elements of White society rather than seeing them as threats to White rule.

It behooves both Whites and Blacks to do this, and if they see themselves as partners, over the course of three generations, the world will see a different Black community in these mixed-race countries.

Black leaders around the world, and peace-loving Whites, should also advocate for more funding to establish centers to teach Blacks self-esteem and worth. Barack Obama's "My Brother's Keeper (MBK) Alliance" program works for the rehabilitation of the Black race. Through that program, opportunities are created for young people of color in the United States to see more value in themselves—and thus start to engage in worthier activities.

Other leaders around the world should follow suit for the underprivileged. Bygone days should be bygone days. Let the inner city wars stop—and let Blacks start all over again. No matter what has transpired, be it remorsefully or not, Africa should reconstitute itself and face the hard reality of competing with those who made the rules of the game and try to beat them at it.

The Chinese on the mainland understood this and went through four decades of self-isolation only to come back stronger than before. The Japanese did the same after World War II. The Germans have rebranded. Africans can do the same if they are ready to sacrifice and work together to build at all levels. The UN and the World Bank should stay neutral and allow for the rebirth of African businesses and creativity. Enough has been seen of imposed White supremacy and racism. This is the time to aspire to see what the world will look like with all the races being equal and living in harmony.

4. Economic Improvement

A closer review of the economic improvement around the world reveals that Africa's biggest problem is its economic performance against other continents. The poor business skills and small scope of businesses fail to trigger the critical mass necessary to create largescale employment.

This situation brings the following areas into focus:

1. Economic Performance
2. Stability of Fiscal Policies
3. Wealth Creation and Innovations
4. Welfare of the Population

4.1. Economic Performance

The World Economic Forum has researched and found out that Africa has low unemployment rates. While this sounds like good news, there is a catch: the values of the services are far less than that of the Europeans and Asians, who do the finishing in the complex supply chains.

Africa's economic activities have been largely agrarian and natural resource-focused. More agriculture, hunting, fishing, mining, carpentry, and related businesses are what Africans focus on, leaving the more rewarding and better-paying jobs to Europeans, Asians, and Americans.

Governments in Black Africa need to dig deeper, listing the factors of production for what they produce and undertaking more activities that are of higher value along the supply chain. For example, I worked as the infrastructure and engineering manager at London Mining Company (LMC). When iron ore was processed at the LMC, it was bought at one hundred dollars per ton when it left Sierra Leone in lumps, and then it was shipped to China and Europe for processing. In the factories of these countries, the raw materials are converted to cast-iron or steel rods and plates and sold back to the same Africans at $400 per ton—not to mention other minerals discovered in the lumps, which come as bonuses to them.

If we take into account the high-paying jobs of the expatriates who work in these mines and the external foreign exchange transfers, it often translates to three to four times the cost of the raw materials. These profits are what bring the income inequality that is widening daily between developed and developing countries.

Africa needs to improve cashing in on the value chain by targeting the high-value components of the chain and not just the handling and processing of raw materials. Professionals with hard bargaining skills are what Africans require to effect this. Industries and governments should be willing to pay good salaries for these positions—and even more so in the early stages.

The good news is that the continent's raw materials—diamonds, gold, and African hard timber—are unique, which is very good leverage in any negotiation. Africans should take advantage of the uniqueness of their situation and not be in a hurry to give anything away at such low prices out of fear of losing the markets.

4.2. Stability of Fiscal Policy

By far, one of the biggest challenges poor Black countries face is maintaining a stable economy. The overreliance on donors is one of the principal causes of this instability. Some economies are so donor dependent that 50–60 percent requires external funding. This means that all planning and development will have to be sanctioned by the powers that be in Washington, London, or Paris. To ensure fiscal stability, inflation of commodity prices and foreign exchange have to be controlled.

Each country needs to develop a sizable amount of reserves to cushion fluctuations in external markets. If I bought cement in 2016 at eight dollars per bag, which is equivalent to thirty-two thousand local currency, then by 2020, it was still eight dollars per bag but eighty thousand in the local currency. For the locals, the price of cement would almost now be 2.5 times in just three years. For the American, the price would remain the same. This means the American would be able to plan his life better than his African counterpart, who only had access to the local currency.

To prevent this, there should be stability in the local currency; countries have to develop reserves of foreign exchange. Botswana achieved this through prudent use of the exports from its diamonds, and ever since, the pula has been a near steady currency.

4.3. Wealth Creation and Innovations

As previously shown, there is this strong nexus between economic status and racism, my so-called economic racism. Therefore, it would seem the Blacks and Indo-Chinese have to create wealth to reduce the stigma of inferiority. Speed in decision-making and projects' implementation is a key factor in this wealth creation.

Delays in decision-making, *procrastination*, is a major problem for Africans. Fear of taking risks is at the core of this. If we consider the time value of money and the fact that the population is growing daily, the only conclusion is to make wealth faster so more people are catered to. The rule of "First to market" should be part of Africa's sales strategy always.

Blacks should see themselves as being on an express train while the rest of the world is on a normal one. More ground needs to be covered within a short time frame if the Black-Yellow-White gaps are to be closed. This also means more hours have to be spent at work or in completing projects.

I developed a simple formula for this in university:

If Work (Effort) x Time Input = Output
The doubling of each input should produce four times the output.
2 x Work (Effort) x (2 x Time Input) = 4 x Output

If you work twice as hard and twice as long, you will achieve four times the normal output. This holds true for many things we do in life. Therefore, more Blacks need to work longer hours on worthwhile and profitable ventures. The change from low productivity jobs in agriculture to high-productivity ones in industry ensures a faster move from poverty to prosperity.

According to the *World Population Review*, the average worker in Africa works less than thirty-five hours per week. This is well below South Korea's or Canada's forty-eight hours per week. Many

Africans and Blacks do not work long hours even though they are stronger genetically and sometimes physically than their Asian counterparts. It has proved that physical work is not all. We need more brains than brawn in Africa to turn things around. And, as shown above, if Blacks can spend more time on work, they are bound to achieve incredible results.

Another Black pioneer of innovation was Lewis Howard Latimer. In 1880, he invented an improved version of the filament used in light bulbs. While Thomas Edison, a White man, is often given the credit, the truth—according to the Khan Academy—is that Latimer made the version that we use today. The Edison version never worked, but because of racism at first, and perhaps because Latimer was Black, his name is often stifled.

Blacks need to be aware that there is a huge potential to change the present impression that nothing good comes out of Africa or from the Black man or woman.

This story about Latimer happened more than a hundred years ago, but a similar story of other Black inventors can still be told today. This can only be possible if the average Black man puts their mind to doing more high-value creativity that will change the dynamics of race relations.

Oprah Winfrey is the world's richest Black woman. She has worked relentlessly to change her image, and she never considers herself inferior to any other human. Today, she has a net worth of around $2.6 billion.

Every Black man and woman can work hard to reduce the global income inequality and social injustice without necessarily being violent. Blacks have been very social and friendly among the races, perhaps to their disadvantage. Being unaware of the exploitative intentions of the other races, the wealth of the continent has been plundered—but this does not have to continue.

Singapore and the four tigers transformed their economies within two generations. African nations need to do likewise. In the schools of Africa, competition on creativity and wealth-creation projects should be intensified. There is too much focus on politics and debating societies, and the science streams are not being funded enough. It is only through scientific breakthroughs that major wealth has been created elsewhere. Ridiculous national annual awards in some countries would have an award for "Best Politician of the Year," while no "Best Inventor, "or "Best Income-Generation Entity," would be awarded.

Oprah Winfrey has been able to utilize television and modern communications gadgets to influence people. Similarly, through major discoveries in science, the industries of the world are producing ten to thirty times the labor-intensive approaches common in Africa. Of course, Africans can change for the better.

5. Welfare of the Population

Africans pray for good health and to be able to feed themselves. Annually, governments in Africa spend 15–20 percent of GDP on agriculture, yet the continent is unable to self-feed its people. With some of the world's most fertile soil and moderate climate, the World Bank estimates that Africa and its Black people will quickly double outputs if the right measures are taken.

Developed nations once mostly relied on strong agricultural bases, which they had transformed into large, mechanized outfits. If Africa is to copy this trend, it needs to create viable economic policies, regulations, and incentive packages. For example, farmers should be given subsidies and internet, cable, satellite TV, cell phone coverage, and road access should also be improved in rural areas to provide for mobility and a continent-wide access.

Africa should have diversified agriculture on a commercial scale to cater to a broad spectrum of clients. These products should include grains, cereals, livestock, and medicinal products—enough to export to frigid countries and temperate countries. By so doing, the continent would generate revenue in foreign exchange. Since some of these require a couple of years to develop, there must be subsidies in the initial years. Five years of continuous support will entrench these sectors.

In the recent past, rainfall in my town was almost four thousand millimeters per year. As a result, lots of homes did not bother with buying treated water in the rainy season. The atmosphere was less polluted, and many homes used the water for laundry and washing clothes and surfaces. Today, the proportion of suspended solids and dissolved air pollutants is increasing. It is becoming increasingly necessary to regulate the consumption of rainwater and ensure the treatment of such water.

Africa needs standards to follow in life, and they must be enforced by every government in Africa.

6. Improving Competitiveness

This is by far the most challenging and demanding factor in the Black-Yellow-White economic competition stage. According to the Global Competitiveness Index, competitiveness is defined as the institutions, policies, and factors that determine a country's level of productivity. In turn, they determine the sustainability of its economic growth and prosperity in the medium to long term.

The desire to be competitive and reduce the income inequality gap is an essential goal for developing countries. However, this has made many successful people look down on the poor. To fully measure competitiveness and develop it further, it has been broken down into twelve pillars in three subsections:

1. The Basic Requirements
2. The Efficiency Enhancers
3. The Innovation and Sophistication Factors

All twelve factors have been discussed already at one point or the other within this book, and the collation now helps us view them in groupings as we prepare to implement them. A strong legal environment is necessary to force industry and businesses to adhere to these standards. All countries need to be competitive in the products they attempt to market to get a fair share of the global market. Africans, and Blacks in general, would take such a fact with a pinch of salt, but the reality is that customers buy products based on quality and performance advantages over other similar products and services.

As a consultant, I have worked on African Development Bank and World Bank contracts. In each of the adverts sent out, there were requirements. For instance, one stated prospective corporate bidders needed to have fifteen years of experience, an annual turnover of $15 million, and have consulted for at least two projects of a similar size. These are requirements that African consultants can hardly meet. As a precondition of "fairness," they go on to require that no preference will be given to bidders based on their country of origin. The donor funds come from these countries with no consideration for local capacity.

On one water infrastructure project, I went through the profile of one such giant, Atkins International (they acquired Howard Humphrey and Sons Consultants) from the UK. Atkins could easily boast of more than fifty projects of a similar nature, and when I looked at the local companies, they barely had two. To resolve such inequalities in competition, they must act as development banks wanting to see their local companies growing quickly to offer more services. The World Bank, African Development Bank, and the Inter-American Development Bank should, in the immediate future, introduce capacity-building measures, requiring that established consultancies and contractors with more than twenty years of experience partner with local companies. They should ensure their participation to take up to 30 percent of the contract sums in all large projects.

If this is implemented, we would see African businesses picking up and providing backstopping for the larger companies. The reason why this is not done is obvious: the fear that Black development could mean the death of Europe. Europe is so technologically advanced that it would take a hundred years for Africans to be as equally competitive. There is therefore really an unfounded fear on the part of Whites. The competitiveness of Black-based economies helps White-based countries have bigger markets in high-tech products.

Despite the above outlook, eight economies in Africa are showing rapid progress in their competitiveness. Ghana, Côte d'Ivoire, Ethiopia, Rwanda, Tanzania, Nigeria, Egypt, and South Africa have well-developed and reliable legal environments, protecting the foreign and local investor. Others are following on.

Competitiveness, in itself, is a crucial phenomenon, which would require an entire book to discuss. However, I will dwell briefly on the key pillars:

1. Standardization
2. Higher Education and Training
3. Infrastructure
4. Market Research
5. Benchmarking
6. Participation in International Organizations

6.1. Standardization

In 2007, a Chinese friend and lecturer of English, made an observation to me. As part of standardization and indirectly creating entry barriers to non-European countries, the EU countries introduced the ISO 9001/2000 standard and the logo CE (*Communauté Européenne*) for products made and to be used in the European Community. I soon realized that all products made in China for the EU market had one or both of these certifications. The Chinese market share improved.

The EU went on to add the Environmental Standards ISO

13000, and most Africans saw this as a wall to the EU market. Instead of complaining, the Chinese companies hired experts in ISO 9001/2000 and ISO 13000, trained them to meet the standards, and certified thousands of companies within ten years. Their products were allowed into the EU once again, and sales boomed in the face of disapproval from some Europeans. China has responded to every potential barrier to new markets by providing the requested standard.

Africa has a lot to gain from China's experience in overcoming trade barriers and economic racism.

6.2. Higher Education and Training

The world is becoming more and more educated every day. With the internet at the disposal of so many people, the speed of computing has increased considerably. Despite the fast pace and reduced costs of internet access, the rate of internet penetration among Blacks is low. The attendance at universities is also low, and Africa's universities are not among the top two hundred in world university rankings.

Africa needs to leverage education if it is to compete globally. Competition brings comparison of standards, and with higher standards, outputs are bound to be higher except in very special local knowledge domains. For example, a Cambridge graduate would always handle modern management better than a Djibouti graduate because of environment and exposure. Infrastructure, availability of research funds, and access to new technology that are used to rank universities around the world are enough reasons for Black and mixed race countries to embark on large investments in Black schools. The universities, technical and vocational educational training (TVET) institutions, and the polytechnics need the human resource base to maintain standards over long periods before they can be ingrained into the system. Poor ethics in examinations management and poor conditions of service for tutors need to be looked into and revised or corrected.

In Sierra Leone, President Dr. Julius Maada Bio runs a platform of free and quality education from primary to secondary schools and has offered free university education to women in the sciences and engineering. The impact can already be seen as the enrollment rate has increased among women, but the infrastructure and equipment to match such enrollment is lacking. More investments are necessary over the next two decades to raise the profile of African universities. The fear is that as soon as there is a change in government, there will be change of focus and education will be dropped from the priority status, reversing the gains of a decade. Oh, that Sierra Leone may continue sustaining free education of her youths for two decades continuously so that we could evaluate the impact of education for developing countries and be an example to other nations.

6.3. Infrastructure

Africa and Black economies cannot compete given the poor state of their economic and social infrastructure. Energy is often seen as the biggest challenge, but the roads, water, irrigation systems, and telecommunications are also old and deficient. Without these five basic elements of infrastructure, industries will find it difficult to grow. If they struggle to do so, their life spans will be short.

The World Bank has often denied support to poor countries to undertake large energy projects, arguing that the economies cannot support the new loans or claiming some environmental condition, in accordance with IFC standards, has not been met. However, some energy projects are known to self-sustain and have recovered costs within the project period. Because there are hidden reasons behind the denial, the funds are often not made available.

This action is similar to the action of the British half a century ago when they held back the development of their colonies, thinking it would hold the colonies hostage forever. As the world economy became more competitive, Britain was no longer able to cash in on its prior advantage with these colonies.

Likewise, the World Bank cannot continually be an impediment to Africa's big projects. In Uganda, when there was opposition to the construction of a six hundred-megawatt power plant, President Museveni decided to seek aid elsewhere. Today, the project is a pride of Africa and is expected to provide electricity for eighty or more years to come.

In Sierra Leone, there was opposition to a three hundred megawatt hydropower plant at Yiben in the north that could bolster the leap to middle-income status. Instead, the country has been highly deficient in electricity supply and remains one of the darkest countries in Africa because the big economies do not believe the country can recover its investment! Now, the CLSG project has been born in which excess power is shared between four countries. Is it late to now invest three hundred million dollars and to recover this in ten to twelve years? It's never late for such an investment?

In summary, apart from its long-term benefits, the development of urban infrastructure in telecommunications, roads, jetties, water, and power can create jobs for the people and spur the continent's development at a much faster rate. Infrastructure development is a must for Africa's economic emergence. Design Build Operate and Transfer, otherwise known as Turnkey schemes and Public Private Partnerships (PPPs) are the new ways to go. In fifteen years, these structures usually revert to national institutions management after the investor would have recouped his investment with profit.

6.4. Market Research

The best way to get a large market share is to understand the market and work out strategies to penetrate it. The world's largest markets are in China, Russia, EU and the United States. The poor Black countries, at this early stage of the new era of transformation of the African image, need to develop a renewed drive to be the preferred supplier for fresh agricultural products in the markets of Europe, the United States, and China while waiting to develop high-tech products.

Chinese companies researched the dos and don'ts of European and American markets and fulfilled the needs of a quality-conscious clientele, thereby succeeding in increasing market share. Equally so, African governments should invest in market research, identify the key penetrating market strategies, and set targets for increased sales. Especially after Covid-19, many farms did not do well in cold countries. A lot of supplies can be done into Europe.

6.5. Benchmarking

Africa is not an island in the global economy. As a continent with 20 percent of the world's population and 50 percent of the world's reserves of natural resources, Africa is a major player in the global field. Africa should leverage this advantage and benchmark developed countries like Japan, India, and Europe in technological development. In a sense, each country should identify its counterpart that is slightly ahead of it in the Human Development Index rankings and benchmark it.

By 2030, Africa is projected to produce only 6 percent of global output. Continentally, its potential should extend to 20 percent, which represents its global population share. If Africa is to earn the respect of the Chinese, the Japanese, and the Europeans as a continent that is ready for business, then this should be the target for every Black man. Quality, respect for delivery schedules, high productivity and reliability should become the new hallmarks of Africa's businesses.

6.6. Participation in International Organizations

International organizations abound in numbers today than have ever existed. They cover a range of social, economic, financial, and technical interventions, including world peace, discrimination, justice, climate change etc. The vanguards among these organizations working for the development of the African continent and its people are the African Union (AU), the United Nations (UN), the African Development Bank (AfDB), and the International Bank for Regional Development (IBRD), which is popularly known as the World Bank (WB).

The meetings of these organizations often attract an assemblage of a huge knowledge base that Africa can tap into. Therefore membership of these institutions and participation in them should not just stop at the ratification of agreements in the national parliaments. There must also be follow-up meetings and concrete actions that are generated from these deliberations. Whether at the UNO, WB, or WEF, a network of professionals can be established to help tap into decades of results from developed countries. Developed countries have a duty of care to ensure that African participants are not left out in subcommittees and working groups.

In turn, African governments must improve their commitment to these protocols and agreements and regularly pay their subscriptions in order to benefit from the outcomes and propel Africa much faster. They must take advantage of opportunities like the climate change carbon funds. Africa barely takes advantage of the hundreds of millions of dollars that are set aside to combat climate change through the Global Environment Facility (GEF) and the Green Climate Fund (GCF).

In 2011, the AU conceived a long-term program, Agenda 63, to guide the continent's vision up to 2063, one hundred years after the creation of the Organization of African Unity (OAU). The AU was formed with a Pan-African vision and African renaissance. We want an integrated, prosperous, and peaceful Africa, driven by its own citizens, that represents a dynamic force in the international arena.

Agenda 63 ends fifty years after its enactment in 2013 and has seven aspirations:

Aspiration 1: A prosperous Africa based on inclusive growth and sustainable development.

Aspiration 2: An integrated continent, politically united and based on the ideals of Pan-Africanism and the vision of Africa's renaissance.

Aspiration 3: An Africa of good governance, democracy, respect for human rights, justice, and the rule of law.

Aspiration 4: A peaceful and secure Africa.

Aspiration 5: An Africa with a strong cultural identity, common heritage, values, and ethics.

Aspiration 6: An Africa whose development is people-driven, relying on the potential of African people, especially its women and youth, and caring for children.

Aspiration 7: Africa as a strong, united, resilient, and influential global player and partner.

Each of these aspirations has goals (twenty in all) to meet the aspirations. The AU ensures all nation members are making progress in these directions. The African Peer Review Mechanism (APRM), an arm of the AU, monitors and evaluates the progress of each country. If all of these goals are developed and met, the Sustainable Development Goals (SDGs) of the UN will automatically and concurrently be brought into focus as living standards improve.

There is a strong correlation between the SDGs and the Agenda 63 goals. According to the Mo Ibrahim Foundation, Agenda 2063 has a distinct focus on democracy, cultural identity, and continental integration, whereas Agenda 2030 (SDGs) has a strong emphasis on climate change-related issues and inequalities. To date, according to the AU, Africa has only achieved an overall 32 percent of the Agenda 63 plans, and some goals are still off track (see figure 8).

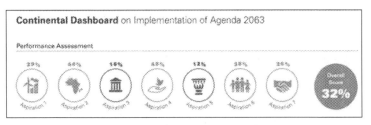

Figure 8: Progress on Agenda 63 by 2019.

The AU has incorporated the New Partnership for Africa's Development (NEPAD) into the African Union's Development Agency (AUDA)'s program. NEPAD was well publicized at its inception, but within five years, its resources were depleted.

In 2010, I tried to interview some lecturers at a university in a West African country. I could not get much from them on the intents and benefits of NEPAD. Even though a decade has passed, very few governments are directly mainstreaming the vision of NEPAD. Only two out of ten persons knew about NEPAD, projects that are supposed to be the Africa Union's flagship.

By making AUDA the technical agency of the AU, charged with implementing the visions of NEPAD, the AU has made a great decision that should have far-reaching impacts on Africans. According to the AU, NEPAD is mandated to facilitate and coordinate the implementation of regional and continental priority development programs and projects and to push for partnerships, resource mobilization and research, and knowledge management.

NEPAD-AUDA will initially focus on:

1. Human capital development (skills, youth, employment, and women's empowerment)
2. Industrialization, science, technology and innovation
3. Regional Integration

4. Infrastructure (energy, water, information communications technology and transport) and trade
5. Natural resources governance
6. Food security

These programs are precisely the areas where major work needs to be done for Blacks to move the continent's development forward.

I suggest that the NEPAD-AUDA provide loan-guarantee facilities for African countries in situations where the AU has validated projects that are in line with AU vision—but with opposition coming from any donor.

A lot of talking has been done over countless cups of sweet African tea and coffee, and some policies have been developed, but faster actions are now required. How much longer should the lower levels of the continent, the masses, stay blind to the fact that only concerted action can achieve the expected results over thirty years?

As it is now, only intellectuals are aware of all these developmental programs. African leaders continue to see their masses as being "unintelligent" and need not be part of the high-level development programs such as NEPAD. This is one of the shortfalls in Africa's development. More citizen participation and consensus building are required at all levels, in all countries, backed by the requisite funding.

I see the work of the former governor of Lagos State, Babatunde Raji Fashola (2007–2015) and that of the governor of Edo State in Nigeria, Godwin Nogheghase Obaseki (born July 1, 1957 in Benin City, Nigeria) and the new Dakar International Airport springing up, or the New Direction government of Julius Maada Bio's work in Sierra Leone on corruption and human capital development. I accept that pockets of people in Africa are getting the message, but the majority must come aboard.

Obaseki focused on six areas: culture and tourism, sports, economic development, environmental sustainability, institutional reforms, infrastructural development, and social welfare. The results are still being felt in the state. Leaders should leave behind a lasting legacy of their tenures and transmit them from one generation to the next by inclusiveness. That ensures sustained development.

Under the AU Agenda 63 and the AUDA-NEPAD, incentives for performance and penalties against nonperformance must be set. The other races have long left the train station, but the Black man is still checking in and will leave in a train of his own.

7. New Approach to Politics

Politics makes governments run. In Africa and most developing countries, governments are the largest single employers and the fastest route to middle-income status for hardworking low-income citizens. Therefore, in Africa, the role of politics is crucial. For the transformation of Africa to be fast and complete, governments must be efficient and—in some cases—transformed. A new approach to politics will look at the following concepts:

1. 1. Inclusiveness
2. 2. Democratic Institutions
3. 3. Reinventing the Government
4. 4. Genuine Intentions to Transform People's Lives

7.1. Inclusiveness

African politics and those of most developing countries have this peculiar characteristic of "winner takes all." This basically means that at the outcome of elections, the winning party only enlists cadre from its membership for national duty. They suppress all other persons who are nonpartisan or non-tribal.

While this "paying the monkey and not the Baboon that worked" situation is far from ideal and effective, it has remained a handy means to keep party members loyal. High-caliber opposition persons have been removed from offices, and highly successful programs have been abandoned because they were initiated by opposition party members.

In the 1960s, Sierra Leone produced good-quality palm oil under the leadership of Sir Milton Margai, a Sierra Leonean, London-trained doctor. By 1967, there was a change of regime, and the opposition APC came to power.

The new leader, Siaka Stevens, ordered all major activities in the Sierra Leone Produce Marketing Board (SLPMB) to be put on hold. Within a decade, Sierra Leone lost its competitive edge, and countries like Malaysia took over and went into full-fledged oil palm production. Today, Malaysia is arguably the world's leading producer of palm oil. Opportunities have been lost in Sierra Leone because local politicians do not think inclusiveness. Continuing successful programs means supporting the agenda of the opposition party and a recipe for losing the next election for lack of originality.

Blacks should try to avoid tribal, ethnic, and political divide and focus on the bigger picture: the national development and refurbishment of the Black image and well-being. One way of ensuring this is by developing a policy that prevents political leaders from making major changes to existing policies. These policies can be identified by independent review committees of the African Union or through an expanded mandate of the African Peer Review Mechanism (APRM). Opposition parties and/ or the electorates can appeal to the APRM to force governments in power to carry on with the unfinished activities of the past government and implement its good policies in order to ensure that there is continuity in government.

7.2. Democratic Institutions

Democracy has been the best-touted system for the human race after theocracy failed in the time of Saul and King David in the Bible. Democracy basically calls for the rule of the law, and that rule is the rule of the people, by the people, and for the people. To ensure that democracy succeeds, strong democratic institutions have to be in place.

In a famous speech, Barack Obama said, "Africa does not need strong rulers but strong institutions" He explained that among those strong institutions are those that guarantee the practice and respect of democracy.

In Africa, the laws and institutions exist, but the willingness to live by them and be governed by them is a major problem. Strong institutions have a top-down approach. Governments have tried to enforce the laws, but institutions should begin to use the bottom-up approach. Instead of strict adherence to the laws of the land, the people should be taught to love their laws and accept the supremacy of the law for the common good. Civic education should be emphasized in all Black countries and communities in the diaspora to ensure citizen participation in all aspects of their communities.

Findel defines civic education as "both formal and informal training given to the citizens to develop in them the knowledge, values, and skills needed for effective participation in the political process and civil society."

Such an idea is not emphasized enough to Blacks in multiracial countries. Even though funds are limited, if multiracial governments spent more on correcting the lack of respect for institutions and other shortcomings, there would be fewer people in prisons.

With citizens abiding by the laws of the land, lawlessness among Blacks would reduce in the United States, South Africa, Jamaica, and Nigeria—and a new Black global profile would emerge.

Africa needs love for the institutions it has created, and it must ensure that these institutions work. In 1996, Sierra Leone published the "National Pledge" as a way of getting more citizens committed to the nation and participating in the democratic process:

I pledge my love and loyalty to my country, Sierra
Leone;
I vow to serve her faithfully at all times;
I promise to defend her honor and good name;
Always work for her unity, peace, freedom, and
prosperity;
And put her interest above all else.
So, help me God. So, help me God.

With God as our helper—and each of us loving the other—Blacks and Whites can live in harmony for the betterment of humanity. In a published paper on civic education, B. A. Adeyemi claimed that the lack of proper civic education in Nigeria is preventing the country's youth from being good national and global citizens. This can also be said of the Blacks in multiracial countries hitherto highlighted. Some are children of immigrants, and some were born in these White-dominated countries. How come they behave differently? Behavioral change is to be a core objective of changing the stereotyping.

7.3. Reinventing the Government

The role of government in Africa's development and the transformation of its image are crucial in bridging the White-Yellow-Black divide.

At a recent workshop in South Africa, Dr. Edward Kamara, a senior monitoring and evaluation officer in the Sierra Leone government, presented a list of factors that affect Afro-based governments. He called it the "Causes of Poor Public Service Delivery" and ranked them in order of importance:

1. Inadequate Citizen Participation/Dictatorships
2. Lack of Skilled Workers
3. Lack of Capacity (Infrastructure, Human and Financial Resources, and Responsiveness to Service Users)
4. Administrative / Political Interference
5. Corruption
6. Lack of Finance or Poor Revenue Base
7. Poor Utilization of Collected Revenue
8. Lack of Modern Facilities
9. Lack of Accountability and Transparency
10. Political Manipulation
11. Poor Documentation
12. Lack of Coordination between Central and Local Government
13. Lack of Administrative Leadership

The foremost factor discussed was lack of citizen participation, which can be attributed to dictatorship. The majority of Black leaders assume absolute power. As such, they make unilateral decisions that affect the lives of those they govern in ways that lead to poor management.

While financial availability can be a major factor influencing the other factors, poor utilization of the little they collect is the root cause of their inefficiencies. The lack of capacity (human and others) to implement development programs is another major factor.

Each year, the intentions are spelled out in national development plans and manifestos. However, evaluations have shown that only 20–40 percent of these plans are implemented at the end, which mainly is due to a loss of focus midstream.

The president of Sierra Leone, Dr Retired Brigadier Julius Maada Bio proudly declared in 2020 that he would achieve most of his manifesto promises during his tenure. It was a big change in African political direction for a leader to take stock of his successes just halfway through his term. To his admirers, it was the first time a Sierra Leonean president could boast of such achievements. He may not be judged by these deliverables at election time, but it's a good start for African democracy.

Political manipulation has resulted in undesirable outcomes from well-conceived projects. Misuse and misappropriation have led to insufficient amenities to implement projects, which has always had disastrous impacts on those who are governed. Redirecting derailed governments is therefore necessary. Once these factors have been identified, each Black government must benchmark the developed countries' democratic achievements and use them to transform their countries. Therefore, Black leaders should accept a new pluralistic approach to governance that ensures better participation.

7.4 Genuine Intentions to Transform People's Lives

Intentions are subjective. No one can read the hidden intentions of people. Winston Churchill said, "Politics is the ability to foretell what is going to happen tomorrow, next week, next month, and next year—and to have the ability afterwards to explain why it didn't happen." This is a way of saying how tricky politics can be. It is also used loosely to mean politicians are liars and tricksters.

My understanding of Churchill's popular political quote is different. It does not necessarily mean politicians have to lie to the people. It means politicians need the acumen to convince people, influence voters, and identify themselves with their political icons. In times of failure, they must be able to explain to their voters why their hopes were not fulfilled.

CONCLUDING REMARKS

Each Black man is challenged. In the motherland, in the United States, in South Africa, in Brazil, in India, in the UK, and in France, there are constant ladders to climb in the corporate world. The Black man does not need to make this worse with debilitating activities, drugs, and violence.

The White man can help with this. Ask White governors are to invest in drug rehabilitation programs for Blacks and provide better support. White Europe and Indo-China have to allow Blacks into senior corporate offices as more and more mixed race children reach such positions. Increase DFIs to Africa and create the enabling environment for the DFIs to be sustainable. Create some of the world's factories in all of Africa—not just South Africa. But first lets have energy and power to support industrial development in Africa. If all the States in the US can be developed and still have unity, why not all of Africa seeing development also and being a part of the World. There has been a myth that if all were developed, the resources of the world would be depleted. I do not subscribe to this theory because, two hundred years ago, man had the same fears. Fifty years ago, we had the same worries about computing. But here we are today, still improving and there's food for all and need for paper more than ever before.

The development of the Black man will in no wise endanger white existence. The White man will just have to learn to do some work on his own. Isn't this all what Do It Yourselves (DIY) are about?

Black leaders can empower their people. All they need is the willingness, the focus, and the perseverance to monitor and attain Africa's goals.

We all need to awake to change Africa's sad narrative.

Awake, Africa! Awake, you Black man, and transform the continent. Awake, you Asian man! Invest from care—and not just for profit. Awake, you White man, and release your neighbor! He can't breathe.

REFERENCES

https://www.britannica.com/topic/race-human/Modern-scientific-explanations-of-human-biological-variation.

https://www.weforum.org/agenda/2020/02/africa-global-growth-economics-worldwide-gdp/.

https://intelligence.weforum.org/topics/a1Gb0000000LGeREAW? tab=publications.

http://www.scielo.br/pdf/psoc/v25nspe/04.pdf - Doctoral Thesis, Ideology Of White Racial Supremacy: Colonization And De-Colonization Processes Ideologia Da Supremacia Racial Branca: Processos De Colonização E Descolonização Simone Gibran Nogueira Zumbi dos Palmares College, São Paulo/SP, Brazil.

https://www.adl.org/education/resources/glossary-terms/ defining-extremism-White-supremacy.

https://en.wikipedia.org/wiki/List_of_ethnic_groups_in_ Myanmar.

https://en.wikipedia.org/wiki/Indigenous_peoples_of_the_ Americas.

https://eji.org/reports/targeting-Black-veterans/ Equal justice initiative.

https://www.culturalsurvival.org/publications/cultural-survival-quarterly/plight-ethiopian-jews 09032020 7:41 pm.

https://www.khanacademy.org/humanities/us-history/civil-war-era/reconstruction/a/life-after-slavery Accessed 15/04/2020.

https://en.wikipedia.org/wiki/British_Empire Accessed 18/04/2020.

https://www.ohchr.org/Documents/Issues/HRIndicators/handbook_governance_statistics.pdf.

Adeyemi B. A., *Content analysis of Civic Education curriculum in senior secondary schools in Osun State*, Nigeria.

Benyera, Everiste, *Reimagining Justice, Human Rights and Leadership in Africa: Challenging Discourse and Searching for Alternative Paths*.

Acemoglu, D., Robinson J., *Why Nations Fail: The Origins of Power, Prosperity and Poverty*, 2012, Profile Books, UK.

Benyera Evariste, *Reimagining Justice, Human Rights and Leadership in Africa*.

Rich, Paul, *Race, Science, and the Legitimization of White Supremacy in, South Africa, 1902–1940*.

Thompson, Leonard M., *A History of South Africa*, Yale University Press, third edition.

Challenging Discourse and Searching for Alternative Paths, Advances in African Economic, Social and Political Development, 2019, Springer.

Toler, Stan, *The Lasting Impact of Positive Leadership*, 2019, Harvest House Publishers, United States.

Printed in the United States
by Baker & Taylor Publisher Services